The Science
of Family

Working with Ancestral Patterns

First published by O Books, 2009
O Books is an imprint of John Hunt Publishing Ltd., The Bothy, Deershot Lodge, Park Lane, Ropley,
Hants, SO24 0BE, UK
office1@o-books.net
www.o-books.net

Distribution in:	South Africa
	Alternative Books
UK and Europe	altbook@peterhyde.co.za
Orca Book Services	Tel: 021 555 4027 Fax: 021 447 1430
orders@orcabookservices.co.uk	
Tel: 01202 665432 Fax: 01202 666219 Int.	Text copyright Nikki Mackay 2008
code (44)	
	Design: Stuart Davies
USA and Canada	
NBN	ISBN: 978 1 84694 200 6
custserv@nbnbooks.com	
Tel: 1 800 462 6420 Fax: 1 800 338 4550	All rights reserved. Except for brief quotations
	in critical articles or reviews, no part of this
Australia and New Zealand	book may be reproduced in any manner without
Brumby Books	prior written permission from the publishers.
sales@brumbybooks.com.au	
Tel: 61 3 9761 5535 Fax: 61 3 9761 7095	The rights of Nikki Mackay as author have been
	asserted in accordance with the Copyright,
Far East (offices in Singapore, Thailand,	Designs and Patents Act 1988.
Hong Kong, Taiwan)	
Pansing Distribution Pte Ltd	
kemal@pansing.com	A CIP catalogue record for this book is available
Tel: 65 6319 9939 Fax: 65 6462 5761	from the British Library.

Printed by Digital Book Print

O Books operates a distinctive and ethical publishing philosophy in
all areas of its business, from its global network of authors to
production and worldwide distribution.
This book is produced on FSC certified stock, within ISO14001
standards. The printer plants sufficient trees each year through
the Woodland Trust to absorb the level of emitted carbon in
its production.

The Science
of Family

Working with Ancestral Patterns

Nikki Mackay

BOOKS

Winchester, UK
Washington, USA

CONTENTS

Preface

How do we define who we are? If someone asked you to describe
yourself what would you say? Maybe you would talk about what
you do for a living, where you live, if you are in a relationship or
have any children. Would you talk about where you are from?
Would you mention your parents? Your Grandparents? In today's
society we don't often think of our family and ancestors as being
connected to who we are as individuals, yet who we are, where
we come from and our place in our family has a huge impact on
not only how we feel about ourselves but also the choices that we
make in our lives. You may be repeating behaviour, acting out
patterns, atoning for actions, looking and waiting for a missing
love or generally carrying the 'stuff' that belongs to your
ancestors all inside you in your life right now. It can be
comforting to think of 'the ancestors' as something quite far away,
unreachable but still there in the background. The reality is it all
starts with your parents, who are connected to their parents, who
are connected to their parents and so on until it all gets a bit
blurry. Patterns, energy, events and burdens from the past are
carried down and are repeated through generations leaving an
emotional, physical and spiritual imprint on the individual as
they follow the fates of those that have gone before. So how do we
make it all better? This book *"The Science of Family"* explores the
idea of family and ancestral patterns, their potential effect and
ways of working with the patterns inherent to your own life. I did
not set out to work with family and ancestral patterns; it is
something that has evolved through the various different aspects
of my work and it has become something I am incredibly
passionate about. Observing and working with these patterns for
myself, individuals and groups has been a common thread
throughout my life whether through my intuitive work with the
Tarot, energy healing, my research as a medical physicist,

through the use of sound work or family constellations. The relationship between science and spirituality is one that I hold close to my heart, I believe they are two sides of the same coin and one cannot exist in its fullness without the other. I have been very fortunate to be able to explore both the scientific and spiritual worlds from an insider's perspective. In the world of family and ancestral patterns I believe the two aspects truly merge. Much has been written of apparent trends within families for physical, mental and behavioural issues however the genetic or physical root has escaped the science world thus far. Perhaps this is because the roots lie within the family and the patterns therein and a combined approach embracing the spiritual as well as the science is called for. By combining these different approaches we can observe the patterns imprinted upon us by our family and our ancestors. We can acknowledge what is and release the burdens of the past and simply take our place. The aim and purpose of *"The Science of Family"* is to share these techniques and observations with you, I have suggested exercises and illustrated the techniques with many examples of my own work. I hope you will be as fascinated as I am and will look to your family and your place within it with fresh eyes, a clear heart and a new passion.When we see it as it really is, and not how we would wish it to be, we are free to move on.

Nikki Mackay
www.flybroomstick.co.uk

Acknowledgements

I would like to thank my teachers, both here and in spirit, who have guided me and pushed me forward. A special thank you especially to David & Gintallia Finlayson-Frost, Jill Purce, Jonathan Goldman, Bert & Sophie Hellinger as well as Leo & the gang.To Stig Hanson who took a risk and a leap of faith on the Reiki research and who pushed me to write the results for publication. Thank you for your support and for supplying the scones & proper coffee in times of stress. Thank you also to Oona and Tir na nOg. To John Hunt for saying yes! A thank you as well to my friends who have supported, supplied chocolate and read 'The book' as it slowly materialised: Nikki, the Lunicorns, Alan, Maarten, Yoda, Agnes – thank you, I couldn't have done it without you! To my ancestors this book is written in your honour. To my family, a huge heartfelt thank you for being simply the best parents, for always being there and believing no matter what tangent I appeared to be going off on. To my partner Ewan for being there, supporting me, believing in me and telling me to just get on with it. Thank you too for your creativity and input. And finally to my son Jasper, thank you for reminding me that the line stretches out before me as well as behind me and that sometimes to truly take your place you need to stop and play in the sand pit for a while.

Chapter 1

Family and Ancestral Patterns

Who we are, where we come from, our roots, our heritage, our lineage, our place in our family has a huge impact on not only how we feel about ourselves but also the choices that we make in our lives. Think of a street, any street, perhaps the street you grew up in. In one house child A grows up in a nurturing and supportive environment where there are no secrets, where everything is open and loving and the child is given the space to be themselves, so perhaps because of this they will grow up with a strong sense of self and a belief in who they are and what they do. Then in the next house there is child B who has to deal with the harsher side of life without the loving support of a connected, nurturing family, experiencing neglect and abuse.Do we expect him to have the same self belief and sense of purpose as child A? Do we accept that perhaps he might make different choices? Next we ponder child C. This is a child who grew up in a home very similar to child A but seems to have a self destruct program in action that just can't be switched off by his loving parents no matter how hard they try. How do we explain that and can we explain that?In our modern society we don't often spend much time thinking about our ancestors and where we come from. We don't often think about why we are the way we are, we are generally too busy living our lives. It is perhaps accepted in our common thinking that the immediate family that we have grown up with, our family of origin, will have an effect in making us who we are but what of the generations further back, what about our ancestors, our family line? It is quite common to have some knowledge of Grandparents but the buck can stop there. Think about your own family for a moment. Do you know where you are from? Do you know your Grandparents? Do you know, really know, your parents? Can you describe who they were, what their struggles through life were, what their relationship with their own parents was like? It is very easy to see the people in our families only in reference to the role they provide to our family or to us as individuals. We start this behaviour with our parents, seeing them as only existing as our parents with no lives before we were born (how funny it is to feel the shift when you become a parent yourself and become plugged in to the family machine) this one-dimensional view of our family members' lives becomes even narrower when it is directed at our grandparents and beyond. However the rich experiences of their lives and their parents' lives are influent upon us whether we like it or not. Their patterns can and sometimes do become our patterns, their strengths our strengths, our choices can unconsciously mimic their choices and very often we try to carry forward that which they started. Sometimes we even carry forward their mistakes and their guilt, or that which is too heavy for them to bear themselves. Is this our place?

A strong awareness of family and the ancestors is however an inherent part of some modern day cultures such as African traditional religions, Indian, Greek, Germanic, China, Japan etc. Often, God is worshiped through communion with lesser deities and ancestral spirits where the living are seen to be placed between their ancestors and those yet to be born. Like various other traditional religions, African traditional religions embrace the natural seasons, the waxing and waning of the moon and the rhythmic pattern of the land. This is not unlike the more pagan past of the Celtic traditions. The more nature based past is something that is slipping back gradually in to the forefront of our mind and as it does so we are remembering things we forgot we had forgotten. As the popularity of the New Age world increases different types of ritual becomes common place among those who seek it. Many of these rituals and traditions are associated with honouring our place in our family line and our ancestors. Spiritual/therapeutic energy healing systems like Reiki have become so popular that they are even starting to find a niche within mainstream healthcare and interestingly the Japanese system of Reiki has a strong lineage element where those teachers and elders that have gone before and paved the way are remembered and honoured. In the Hawaiian Huna tradition *Aumakua* are perceived as ancestral spirits - who can help their descendents if asked. Traditional rituals such as the Native Americans Sweat Lodge are now openly accepted, at least in a workshop context, in the sweat lodge the Spirits and ancestors where both physical ancestry (your blood line or family line), and energetic ancestry (teachers/helpers/guides) are remembered, honoured and aligned with. What happens after the workshop ends and we all go home? Do we remember the essence of what we have learned and experienced? Do we remember that which we reconnected to that we didn't know we knew? Perhaps it is more comfortable for our sense of the ancestors to be something that is very far away and hard to reach.It is also commonly accepted that you can inherit genetic/biological predispositions from your family and is anecdotally accepted that you inherit to some degree your talents, gifts and foibles from that same family line so is it that far a stretch to consider that perhaps we carry some of the burdens and baggage from those who have gone before us? That we perhaps carry forward and perpetuate patterns of behaviour, physical conditions and emotional responses. Imagine if we could see what influence these patterns were having on our life. Imagine also if we could choose to nip a particular pattern in the bud, refusing to perpetually carry it forward to the next generation. Imagine the effect that might have...In highlighting some of our family and ancestral patterns we can start to illuminate the reasons behind why we are the way we are and why we choose the things we choose. The information gleaned will not only shed light on the dynamics and entanglements of our family of origin and, if appropriate, our subsequent created family, but can also have a significant impact on our emotional and physical state. The idea that physical symptoms are manifestations of psychological pain is not a new one and there has been much written about so-called psychosomatic illnesses. There has also been some research investigating certain behavioural patterns within families such as family histories of suicide, alcoholism and drug addiction. It is now well established that a family history of suicide indicates that an individual is at raised risk for suicidal behaviour. In fact a family history of suicidal behaviour has been noted to be associated with suicidal behaviour at all stages of the life cycle, including those over 60, and across psychiatric diagnoses (reviewed in *Roy, Nielson, Rylander et al., 2000*). This is also the case for those that self-harm and suffer from mood disorders, mental health issues or depression.A research study in to substance abuse found that everyone with a family history of alcoholism is at risk for developing alcohol abuse disorders, but males are at the greatest risk, according to research at the Behavioural Sciences Laboratories."The development of alcoholism among individuals with a family history of alcoholism is about four to eight times more common than it is among individuals with no such family history," said William R. Lovallo, Director of the Behavioural Sciences Laboratories at the Veterans Affairs Medical Centre, Oklahoma City and corresponding author for the study. "Although the definition of 'family history' is different according to different researchers, we define it as when either or both of the person's parents have had an alcohol problem."(*William R. Lovallo et al.* May 2006.)Research has also shown that male gender and behavioural dis-inhibition are strong predictors of alcohol problems.Researchers in to both fields of study (suicide and substance abuse) agree that there is scientific evidence that alcoholism/suicide/addiction has a family component, but the actual gene that may cause it has yet to be identified. Perhaps the pattern is not a genetic one but instead an ancestral one.exploring Ancestral and Family patterns through techniques such as energy healing, tools such as the Tarot or Family Constellation work enables us to bring clarity to some of the threads running through our lives and the lines within our family. Issues surrounding physical symptoms, chronic illnesses and attitudes towards our body, can be looked at within the context of our family, our history, and the influences around us helping us to see the deeper level at which interconnectedness happens. This awareness helps bring to the foreground what the purpose of the symptom or pattern of behaviour is there for, bringing clarity to issues that perhaps have been weighing on us for quite some time, which frighten us, irritate us, damage us or befuddle us. Once we have this information we can then do something about it. Again this idea I'm putting forward that we are tapping in to something that we know, we just don't know that we know, is not necessarily a new one. Carl Jung's concept of the Collective Unconscious, Rupert Sheldrake's theory of the Morphic field and even borrowing from the popular trend of quoting the "new quantum mechanics" and their zero point field theory, all of these hypothesis have the basic foundation of an inter-connectedness between all things. Above all everyone has his of her own place in their family system and it is important to be acknowledged within that place. Very often there is at least one member of the family who is unconsciously not seen by other family members and this is where the problems start and the root of many patterns. The "system" or what is known as the 'family field' wants the family to remember the forgotten member. This entanglement can be highlighted through family and ancestral working and then brought back to a state of balance. Events or situations which can have an impact on the family system, which can cause members of the family to be excluded or to not be seen, are many and far reaching. It is not necessarily the events alone which trigger the initial change within the family system and becomes a pattern effecting future/current generations but also it is the way in which the event or entanglement is handled by the family itself. The acknowledgement of how things are, how they really are and the repercussions of the event is really the key issue.

I have highlighted below some common examples of events that can perpetuate themselves into a degenerative pattern:

- Early death of one of the parents
- Rejection of parent/child
- Early death of a child (also miscarriage, abortion, still-birth)
- Serious accidents, traumatic events, murder or suicide
- Situations involving war and violence
- Guilt (connected to crime/inappropriate behaviour/helplessness)
- Roots in different countries (countries different to the country of origin)
- Behavioural patterns such as drug/alcohol addictions
- Adoption
- Previous marriages or engagements that haven't been acknowledged or given a place

As you can see there is probably at least one example on the list that will apply to most people. Have a think about your own life and the lives of your family members. Do you already have little warning bells ringing in your head? Are you aware of some of the patterns that might be at play in your own life? The root cause of the particular pattern is not always that obvious from the outside or from first glace. Whether the pattern involves a propensity for a particular type of relationship (be it romantic, working or platonic), a self-sabotaging trait such as alcohol or drug abuse, a physical issue (issues around fertility and childbirth can be particularly prevalent in family patterns), suicide within families, physical ailments or a sense of duty beyond reason to stick to a particular career when all is screaming inside for something different, once the pattern or entanglements have been highlighted there are a number of ways of clearing the pattern to bring balance once more. It is the acknowledgement of the pattern and the events and *seeing* and accepting things the way the really are, not how we would like them to be, that is the key. In the following chapters I will discuss different ways in which you can work with your family and ancestral lines to renew and reconnect to your place within your family. It is not always easy to look at where we come from but sometimes there is a need to go back before you can move forward. I will be discussing examples of this work in action and giving suggestions and exercises to try yourself. If you are already sitting thinking that this work resonates with you then please take your time to work through the exercises as we progress together.

Chapter 2

Energetic Imprint of Ancestral Patterns

My memories when I think back to my undergraduate days as a physicist are not of the lectures and laboratories but of the student counselling service that I worked for and eventually became a trainer for. When I completed my first degree it seemed like a natural progression to move in to the field of medical physics. Combining science with healing and working with individuals was a big draw for me and the strong research element to the post was an added bonus. The few years I spent working within the healthcare sector were certainly challenging in and of themselves, my rose tinted view of working in the healing profession was soon brought sharply in to focus. It also coincided with the time that I first discovered energy healing and the concept of working with 'energy' to bring balance to an individual. Reiki is non-invasive treatment that can complement existing allopathic treatment, carries no side effects and no contra-indications, and appears to reduce stress, help boost the immune system and stimulate the healing process within the body. I must admit to being somewhat sceptical when I first heard about Reiki and other energy healing systems. How could you possibly have an effect on someone's health by simply waving your hands over them? When I mentioned this to a friend they simply held their hands over mine and I was gobsmacked that I actually could feel something. This had to be investigated. I decided to book myself in for a couple of sessions and found them to be hugely beneficial. I had experienced M.E. (myalgic encephalomyelitis) as a teenager, interestingly enough around the time of my budding interest in the Tarot and all things esoteric and it had a tendency to rear its head if I was under a lot of stress or just not looking after myself properly. After I experienced a few Reiki healing sessions and felt it for myself I became convinced of its value as a healing and spiritual tool. I also became convinced that something that causes you to feel relaxed, to improve your health and wellbeing in such a positive and tangible way must have some physiological effect within the body. I was certain that this couldn't just be due to a psychological belief. I came to the conclusion that if there was an actual physiological effect of the energy healing that this would be triggered within the nervous system, and more specifically, the Autonomic Nervous System (ANS). The ANS is concerned with the functions of the body that we ourselves cannot control directly such as respiration, blood pressure, sweating and vaso-dilation. I started to investigate previous research into energy healing to see if anyone else has come up with this link. I discovered that there have been several attempts to study the mechanism of effect in touch therapies such as Reiki, however most have been anecdotal in approach and few studies have used a rigorous scientific approach for the measurement of biological outcomes. A review of previous studies showed an apparent link between Reiki treatment and the autonomic nervous system. One of the most commonly reported effects of Reiki is that of relaxation or a reduction in stress. The ANS is the motor system for emotion; if Reiki were to ameliorate stress it would therefore also have some effect on the ANS. It just so happened that at that time I had just finished a rotation period working in the Institute of Neurological Sciences at the Southern General Hospital in Glasgow, a world-class centre for research of this type. I contacted my supervisor at the institute to discuss my ideas about energy healing and the ANS and to propose a plan for a research study. He was as curious as I was, and so we began to put together a proposal. It took considerable time, effort and energy on our part before we were finally given approval to go ahead with the study, which we entitled "An investigation into the effect of Reiki on the Autonomic Nervous System"(*N. Mackay et al,*

2004). The aim of our study was to investigate if some indices of autonomic function would show any significant differences between Reiki treatment, a placebo treatment and a control group. Eight different physiological parameters were recorded: heart rate; systolic blood pressure; diastolic blood pressure; mean blood pressure; cardiac vagal tone; cardiac sensitivity to baroreflex; skin temperature and respiration rate. From the statistical analysis of the data we found that there were no significant differences present in the control group, this was as expected. However we did find statistically significant differences between the Reiki and placebo groups, namely changes in heart rate and blood pressure. For those who received Reiki treatment, there was a significant reduction in heart rate and diastolic blood pressure that did not appear in either the placebo or the control group. This suggests that perhaps the difference in blood pressure has been caused by higher centres within the nervous system setting a different control level in Reiki but not in placebo. So what does all this actually mean? Scientifically, what we can say after carrying out this study is that there appear to be significant differences between the Reiki group and placebo and control groups. The nervous system appears to be responding differently to Reiki than to placebo Reiki which strongly indicates that Reiki has some effect on the autonomic nervous system. What we can say after completing this study is that the body, and the ANS specifically, responds to Reiki or energy healing and that this response is not purely a psychological effect or wishful thinking on the part of practitioner and/or patient.

I worked quite intensively with Reiki and other forms of energy healing, such as SKHM and sound healing, during this period. I have to say at this point that I am not a huge fan of breaking energy healing down into different types with one being of a "higher vibration" than another and therefore being more effective. As far as I am concerned energy is energy and the effect has more to do

11

with the intention behind the application rather than the particular system a practitioner is following. An interesting study by Fred Sicher & Elizabeth Targ et al (*A Randomised Double-Blind Study of the Effect of Distant Healing in a Population with Advanced AIDS 1998*) looked at the effect of distant healing on AIDS patients during a six month double blind study. They randomly assigned a patient group of forty people with advanced AIDS in to two different groups. One of the groups received distant healing along with their regular care (they were not told which group they were in). Forty healers from various different geographical locations were selected and the healing methods they practised ranged from Christian, Jewish, Buddhist, Shamanic, meditative and bio-energetics. Each of the subjects in the study received distant energy healing for one hour a day for six days from a total of ten different healers over a ten-week period. After the study was concluded they noted that the patients receiving the energy healing had significantly fewer outpatient visits and hospitalisations, less severe illnesses and complications and an improved mood. This study is an excellent example of the efficacy of energy healing and underlines the point that it is the intention that is important not the particular 'brand' of healing that you work with.

In working so solidly with energy healing in some of its different guises for a concentrated period of time and, after the research was published, going on to leave my post as a Clinical Physicist to set up a Holistic Centre meant that I spent more time teaching, using energy healing and intuitive Tarot session as a therapeutic tool. This created an excellent space for observing some of the less obvious effects of this type of work. I started to notice correlations between the emotional, behavioural or physical patterns affecting an individual and where stagnant, blocked or missing energy areas appeared in their energetic field or actual physical body. The more I worked with it the more specific the observations became and I started to combine my intuitive Tarot sessions with the energy healing sessions as this seemed to give a more rounded approach and have a more beneficial outcome for the individual. Not only could the patterns in their life having an effect at the present time be highlighted but together we could also locate where in their body this pattern was being held and we could work to release that. I started to notice the presence of the family lines coming through as well and was able to discern the greater ancestral and family influence upon the situation. There gradually appeared to be a system of ways in which the family or ancestral memories and events are stored within the physical or energetic bodies, by utilising this system along with the intuitive and healing techniques I really felt like I'd taken a huge jump forward in my understanding of ancestral patterns and how to work with them.

The Bodies' Energetic Field

When working with individuals I started to notice that there was a marked difference between how different areas of the body feel. I say the "feel" of the energy and what I mean by that is my sense or perception of the individual's energetic body, also known as their aura. There has been a surprising amount of research carried out over the years looking at the existence of the subtle bodies within the aura. It is generally scientifically accepted that we have a physical 'aura' surrounding our bodies. This is made up of energetic fields, a combination of electromagnetic fields, low frequency radiation, infrared and electrostatic energy radiating from our bodies. Auras first appeared in western writing around 2600 years ago when they became incorporated into the Pythagoreans' teachings. Ancient rock carvings and paintings depict crude images of energetic fields around the head area. Images of holy people also show them with an aura or halo surrounding them. It is commonly accepted that the aura is the home to the universal life force of energy which flows through us all.Paracelsus a Swiss philosopher-physician in the 1500's was one of the first people in the west to write about the aura. He believed that there was a vital force that "radiates within and around living beings like a luminous sphere". The physicist, Sir Isaac Newton, has also been loosely linked with aura research because of his work with the composition of white light and his discovery of the effect of passing white light through a prism. In1908 Dr. Walter Kilner developed a process that enabled humans to 'see' the aura using a screen containing two plates of glass with a small gap between them. The gap was filled with dye allowing people to view the ultra violet spectrum. His research was ridiculed by the scientific community, however Kilner believed that any doctor could use his screen as a scientific tool as areas of disease would show up as dark patches within the aura. In the late 1930s a Russian scientist, Seymon Kirlian, accidentally discovered how to photograph the aura. He is said to have observed a flash of light between a patient's skin and an electrode when the patient was receiving shock treatment at a psychiatric institution. He then went on to develop the technique known as Kirlian photography. The Kirlian technique doesn't actually use a camera, the object being photographed is normally placed between two metal plates that are oscillating at a specific frequency, photos of fingers or hands are created by placing the part that is to be photographed against film that is held against a charged metal plate. Some research has recently been carried out looking in to the efficacy of Kirlian photography as a tool for detecting the aura "Kirlian photography and its derivatives may be useful as a research tool by providing visual records of complex bodily responses to experimental situations. For example, responses to physiological or psychological stressors." (*Tim Duerden et al.* 2004).Now you can also have photos supposedly of your aura taken at many psychic fairs around the country and have them interpreted by a psychic. Again these photos are not a true image of the aura field. The cameras used are electronically creating the aura rather than photographing it. In general they work by attaching sensors to the skin of the person being photographed, the electrical resistance is then measured and pattern of colours in generated around the image of the body according to the strength of resistance. The colours are assigned according to field strength and resistance not by what is actually 'seen'.

Masculine & Feminine Energy

When working with others it is quite common to feel that specific points in the body draw more energy than others do. The aura is purported to be made up of several different overlapping and interacting layers which correspond to different aspects of our being. The following is an example of the different layers within the aura, although opinions do differ: The **physical body** is our first body, and the one we are all familiar with. The **ethereal body** is the second body (the first energetic body), and follows the shape of the physical body closely. It is supposed that this field channels emotions, thoughts and intuitions from the higher auric bodies, and contains the life force energy that nourishes the physical body. The **astral or emotional body** is the second energetic body and carries within it our emotions and our personality traits. The **mental body** contains our rational thoughts, our ideas and beliefs. The **spiritual body** is our fourth energetic or conscious body. This is the immortal energy body, which connects us to the divine.Some people can see auras quite naturally, others may spend years working to catch a glimpse of colour, but we are all capable of developing our perception of energy fields, be it through our visual sense, our physical awareness of energetic sensations, or an intuitive feel for the energy surrounding people, objects and places. When first working with energy, all you really need to know is that the aura is there. We are all aware of our own and others' energy fields to some extent: when you feel uncomfortable with someone standing too close to you, or pick up "vibes" – good or bad – from someone, then you are sensing their aura. When you work with the aura, even with your hands several inches from another's body, you can sense certain areas that just feel different - hot, cold, jaggy, 'fizzy', empty etc. Through scanning (moving your hands through the air, a few inches from the body and following its contours, noting any change in sensation) the aura before I began working with someone the more I became aware of these differences in the energetic fields. One of the first things I noticed was that there was a marked difference between the left and right sides of the energetic fields and that if I allowed myself to connect with that I was able to intuit information about the individual's family lines. One individual that I worked with, Sarah, came to see me as she was feeling low and a little depressed. When I started to scan her aura with my hands I noticed that the left side of her body felt almost like it was nailed down to the table but the right side was fizzy and cold. It felt to me that the left side was connected to her Mother's line and she felt very burdened, whereas the Father's line felt almost as if it didn't exist. There was also a strong 'blocking' sensation around her lower abdomen. When I shared this with her during the session she explained that her Mother had recently suffered a stroke and that she was caring for her, they had been estranged for a number of years and she was finding it very difficult as the Mother had kept her Father's identity a secret until after his death. We managed to release some of the energy associated with this that had been held in her body allowing her some relief by acknowledging her emotions.

After experiencing a number of sessions with the obvious presence of ancestral lines and other markers in the energetic body I decide to research links between emotional experiences and the physical body. The idea that physical symptoms are manifestations of psychological pain is not a new one. Upon doing a little digging I found out that different systems of belief assign masculine and feminine qualities to the subtle energies within and around the body. The Tibetan Buddhist system believes that the masculine body corresponds to our right hand side and the feminine to our left. According to the Tibetan teachings, after the last breath, the subtle energies of the body draw toward the heart area. This subtle energy that maintains the white, masculine energy, received from the father at the moment of conception and stored in the crown of the head, moves down toward the heart. The deceased is said to have a visual experience like moonlight at this point. Then the red, feminine energy received from the mother at conception and stored below the navel, rises toward the heart. The deceased then has a visual experience of redness, akin to the sky sunrise or sunset. The masculine and feminine energies merge as you slip into unconsciousness. This detection of illness or injury within the auric field can actually be explained. As we discussed previously, the body is constantly emitting waves of low level radiation, electromagnetic energy and when the body is healthy these waves are emitted coherently or in phase, however when we are ill or injured the part of the physical or subtle body affected will emit these waves chaotically and it is this chaotic emission that you are 'feeling' for. When you connect to any healing energy and *intend* that you are sending this energy to an individual the energy is transmitted in waves from your hands. When these strong, coherent, in phase waves meet the chaotic and incoherent waves of energy being emitted from the individual they start to bring them back in phase. This can have an immediate effect though in chronic cases depending on the nature of the ailment it may take many sessions before any progress is made.

Our Karmic History

The spinal column and the psychic-energetic column it is purported to hold, has many myths and traditions surrounding it from karmic encoded DNA to Kundalini energy. The philosophical explanation of karma can differ slightly between traditions, but the general concept is basically the same, through the law of karma, the effects of all deeds actively create our past, present and future, making us responsible for our own life, as well as all that it brings to both ourselves and others. In religions that incorporate reincarnation, karma extends through our present life and all past and future lives as well and some also include our ancestry. Kundalini is believed to be a psycho-spiritual energy, the energy of the consciousness, which is thought to reside within the sleeping body, and is aroused either through spiritual discipline or spontaneously to bring new states of consciousness, including mystical illumination. Kundalini is Sanskrit for 'snake' or 'serpent power', and it is believed to lie like a serpent at the base of the spine. The importance of the energy of the spinal column is also found in Japanese heritage in traditional Reiki systems. Sekizui Joka Ibuki-ho – is a method of cleansing the spinal cord with breath. Spinal cord cleansing is believed to help to purify your karma. According to Koshin-do, karma is recorded in the spinal cord. Through spinal purification, stagnant energies from the past are cleared and the person is filled with Universal life force. This animates the cells within the body and allows us to remember our connection to our ancestors. Sekizui means, 'spinal cord, spinal'; Joka means, 'purification, cleanse, exorcise'; Ibuki means 'breath'; and Ho means, 'method, technique or way'.By simply scanning the length of the spinal column or by placing one hand at the base of the spine and one hand at the crown of the head it is possible to gain a clearer energetic impression of an individual's ancestral patterns. Very often when you work in this way with an individual you will perceive the information on the areas of pain, stagnation or blockages within your own body. This can be related to chakras or to points on the meridians that are close to the skin. The word chakra comes from the ancient Indian language of Sanskrit and means 'wheel' or 'vortex'. The traditional Hindu system names seven major chakras. Indian mystics and yogis have had knowledge of the concept of the seven maps of consciousness embedded into the spinal column from the coccyx to the crown of the head since around 2,500BC. Chakras are perceived to be spinning vortexes of energy, each of the seven vibrating at a different rate each one being associated with different colours, sounds, emotions and organs etc. In a healthy body and mind the energy flowing through these chakras is perfectly balanced, as is the energetic connection between them. Any imbalance in the mind or body will impact the chakras, as they contain an imprint of every emotionally or physically significant event you have been through as well as the connection to the family and ancestral lineage. Energy blocks from one chakra to another can manifest themselves in internal conflicts, such as the classic war between the head and the heart as well as physical and emotional issues.

Root Chakra

The root chakra is positioned at the base of the spine and pubic bone; it is traditionally red in colour.This chakra represents our roots encompassing our family values, our ancestral line and fundamental beliefs. How we relate to our parents and our ancestors and in turn how we relate to our basic material needs along with our sense of "belonging" and our place within our family. Our ability to survive and prosper in the world is "rooted" within this chakra as the relationship with our parents defines our ability to achieve on all levels.

Sacral Chakra

The sacral chakra is positioned in the lower abdomen and is traditionally associated with the colour of orange. Our sense of belonging, desires, drive and ambition have strong connections with this energy centre. The roots of addictive behaviour and self-destructive patterns can also be found here as this is a link to the Father's ancestral lineage. When the Father (or other strong male from the masculine line) is missing, detached or rejected then this energy centre is weakened. Our issues and burdens about ourselves and others are potentially carried here. Also can affect how we relate and communicate our needs to others.

Solar Plexus Chakra

The solar plexus chakra is to be found between the navel and the base of the sternum. This is the storage point for the judgements, opinions and beliefs that we have about the world and ourselves and is also the storage place for our will and willpower. Energy associated with our Mother's lineage and the burdens from that line are carried here. A rejection of the Mother or that line will result in a weakening of this energy centre affecting our ability to drive forward our life successfully.

Heart Chakra

The heart chakra is positioned at the centre of the chest and is associated with the colour green in many traditions. This chakra is seen as the centre of the human body and the connecting point between the higher and lower chakras – the co-existence of body and spirit. It is also the point at which the masculine and feminine ancestral lines find a point of balance and harmony. If however there is an imbalance or heavy entanglement in either or both of the ancestral lines then this energy centre will be impacted by that. This will in turn impact on our emotional, physical, mental and spiritual wellbeing. Thus affecting our feelings of unconditional love, forgiveness, compassion and our ability or inability to relate to those around us. It is also the emotional centre where we unconsciously store the experiences of our ancestors.

Throat Chakra

The throat chakra is quite naturally to be found at the throat at the base of the neck and is traditionally linked with the colour blue.This chakra is known as our "seat of responsibility" and through our throat chakra we say "yes" or "no" to life's options. It is also seen as a vehicle for the soul's expression of its desires and our ability to define ourselves in the world. As such it is linked strongly to the energy of our siblings both born and unborn. If a sibling has been excluded from the family (examples of this would be through abortion, miscarriage, adoption etc) and continues to be excluded and unacknowledged then this impacts how the remaining siblings feel about their "place" within the family system.

Third Eye Chakra

The third eye chakra is traditionally associated with the colour purple or indigo and is positioned in the middle of the forehead.This chakra is our inner and outer visual centre. Through it we obtain symbols, colours and pictures that represent our reality, our feelings about ourselves, our place and our goals. This can become clouded with the feelings or goals of those that have gone before us. This chakra has strong links with the ancestors in the realm of the dead, the realm where our ancestors cross to be at peace. This can either be a positive or negative connection, if there is an ancestor or strong entanglement that has not been resolved or acknowledged then the ancestor(s) and any victims will still be influent upon us as if they were still alive. Through this chakra they will link in with our reality and we will be drawn to them, especially if we do not have a strong rooting through our parental lines. At the opposite end of the spectrum positive guidance and love can come through the connection to the ancestors at peace in the realm of the dead through this particular energy centre.

Crown Chakra

The crown chakra, as the name suggests, is positioned at the crown of the head and is associated with white light. The crown chakra is seen as the centre of our divinity and our connection with the divine source and is the receptive means for us understanding our path and our purpose. This is also our point of connection with our children or unborn children.By scanning the body and taking particular note of the areas that stand out or feel different we can begin to assemble an energetic picture of how an individual's ancestral and family experiences, patterns and burdens have been integrated in to who they are. There are some fairly obvious correlations from the chakra system to the effects of family systems. An individual who is not in a place of strength within their family, not fully themselves, will very often when scanned feel as if they have no root or energy around their feet. Information on why this is can be gleaned from the Masculine and Feminine aspects of the energetic bodies as well as any other blockages or anomalies that are present within their field.

Scanning your own Energetic Body

It is also possible to scan your own body to enable you to highlight the areas in your body that link back energetically to your family and ancestry allowing you to perhaps have a bit of an energetic clear out. It would be useful to either read through the exercise a few times before you try it, to record it (again leaving sufficient space for your own personal exploration) or to have a friend read it aloud for you.

1. It's probably best to be lying down for this exercise, make sure that you are comfortable and warm before you start. You may need a blanket as your body temperature may drop when you are relaxed.
2. Spend a moment relaxing and focussing your awareness on your physical body. Allow your breath to flow naturally and quietly observe the sensations in your own body.
3. Focus on your feet, feel the surface upon which your feet rest. Visualise roots growing out of the centre of the soles of your feet. Feel these roots burrowing through the floor upon which you are standing, through the foundations of the building, down into the earth. Imagine the roots growing deeper and deeper until they reach the centre of the earth. Feel yourself connected to the earth through your feet and then start to draw up the warm earth energy. Draw it up through your feet

and feel it spreading upwards through your body.

4. Now visualize your Root chakra as a red ball of light around the base of your spine. Feel the energy of the ball of light pulse there.

5. Now begin to gently tune in to this ball of white light in your mind. Noticing how it feels, any emotions or pictures that come to your mind's eye as you link in. Notice also if any other areas of your body draw your attention as you focus on your root.

6. Now turn your attention to your sacral chakra. Imagine a glowing, spinning orange coloured ball. Again noticing how it feels, any emotions or pictures that come to your mind's eye as you link in. Allow yourself to relax and sink in to the experience.

7. When you are ready to move on bring your focus to your solar plexus chakra. You will see a glowing, spinning yellow coloured ball of light. Again noticing how it feels, any words, feelings or images that come to you.

8. Now turn your attention to your heart chakra. This time the ball of light changes to a soft green colour. How do you feel connecting with this chakra? What if any emotions or pictures come to your mind's eye as you link in. Allow yourself to relax and breathe as you focus on your heart. You may sense that some chakras are quite restricted, and if need be, you can visualize them opening up, receiving energy from above until you are able to connect with them.

9. When you are ready to move on bring your focus to your turn your attention to your solar plexus throat chakra. You will see a glowing, spinning blue coloured ball of light this time. Again noticing how it feels, any words, feelings or images that come to you. You may feel that you need to speak aloud at this point and if so it is important to allow yourself the space to do so.

10. Now turn your attention to your third eye chakra. Imagine a

glowing, spinning brilliant indigo coloured light. Notice how it feels, any emotions or pictures that come to your mind's eye as you link in. You may see images that seem familiar, allow yourself to relax and sink in to the experience.

11. When you are ready gently notice how the energy is moving upwards again and spreading to your crown chakra at the top of your head. You will see a pulsing ball of pure white of gold light. Notice how it feels, any emotions or pictures that come to your mind's eye as you link in. You may see images that seem familiar, allow yourself to relax and sink in to the experience.

12. Slowly bring your awareness back to your body, to your surroundings, wiggle your fingers and toes, and open your eyes gently.

Take some time to record your experience and note any areas that felt stuck or uncomfortable. Also take note of the areas or chakras where you felt you had a particularly strong or flowing connection.

A useful way of exploring the ancestral roots of any areas that did feel stuck or uncomfortable is to focus your energy on the third eye chakra and the occipital ridge at the back of your head.

The occipital ridge is believed to be the seat of your soul and also a direct connection to your ancestral energy and family line. By holding your non-dominant hand over the occipital ridge and your dominant hand over your third eye chakra you will be able to stimulate the flow of energy between these two important points. By setting aside some time to regularly work with these two points, and any other chakra that feels uncomfortable, you will not only gain some insight in to the root cause of the issue but also start to clear the stagnant energy from your chakra system.

The Heart of it All
At this point I decided to revisit the research that I had previously

completed on energy healing and look in greater detail at how the body physically reacted to the six different hand positions of the eyes, temples, occipital ridge, heart chakra, knees and the soles of the feet. As I mentioned previously there were statistically significant changes within the Reiki group in the heart rate and the diastolic blood pressure measurements, there were also significant changes in the cardiac vagal tone (CVT) and the cardiac sensitivity to baroreflex (CSB). The CVT is an indicator of parasympathetic response which in general causes a decrease of autonomic activity such as a decrease in heart rate, i.e. the relaxation response. The CSB is an indicator of sympathetic activity which generally causes an increase of activity in the end organ such as an increase in heart rate. In the study the CVT response increased and the CSB decreased working together to create the relaxation response within the bodies ANS resulting in the observed reduction in heart rate and diastolic blood pressure. I decided to have a closer look at the four measurements of HR, DBP, CVT and CSB in order to observe any difference in response to the six different hand positions used. The data I looked at was the statistical analysis of the responses recorded from the initial baseline measurements. The analysis is illustrated below (*Figure 1 – Heart Rate Response*).

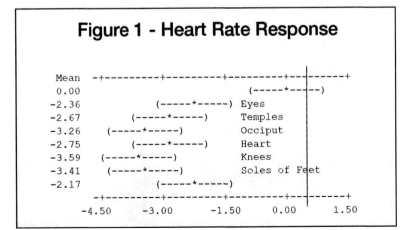

```
Figure 1 - Heart Rate Response

Mean    -+---------+---------+---------+---+------+
0.00                                  (-----*---+--)
-2.36                   (-----*-----) Eyes
-2.67             (-----*-----)       Temples
-3.26         (-----*-----)           Occiput
-2.75             (-----*-----)       Heart
-3.59       (-----*-----)             Knees
-3.41       (-----*-----)             Soles of Feet
-2.17             (-----*-----)
        -+---------+---------+---------+---+------+
     -4.50      -3.00      -1.50      0.00      1.50
```

You can see that the heart rate was reduced gradually from the hand positions over the eyes, temples and occipital ridge but rises again at the heart chakra.

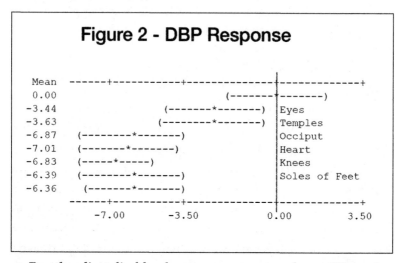

```
              Figure 2 - DBP Response

Mean   ------+-----------+---------------+-------------+
0.00                                 (-------*-------)
-3.44                       (-------*-------)  Eyes
-3.63                       (--------*-------)  Temples
-6.87     (--------*-------)                   Occiput
-7.01     (-------*-------)                    Heart
-6.83     (-----*-----)                        Knees
-6.39     (--------*-------)                   Soles of Feet
-6.36       (-------*-------)
       ------+-----------+---------------+-------------+
          -7.00       -3.50          0.00         3.50
```

For the diastolic blood pressure you can above (*Figure 2 – Diastolic Blood Pressure Response*) see that the greatest reduction occurs between the occipital ridge, the heart and the knees.

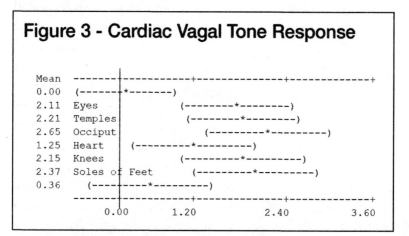

```
Figure 3 - Cardiac Vagal Tone Response

Mean   ------+-----------+---------------+-------------+
0.00   (------*-------)
2.11   Eyes            (--------*--------)
2.21   Temples         (--------*--------)
2.65   Occiput           (---------*---------)
1.25   Heart    (---------*---------)
2.15   Knees           (---------*---------)
2.37   Soles of Feet     (---------*---------)
0.36   (----+----*---------)
       ------+-----------+---------------+-------------+
          0.00        1.20           2.40         3.60
```

The cardiac vagal tone increases from the eyes, temples and the occipital ridge but drops again at the heart centre. This is shown above (*Figure 3 – Cardiac Vagal Tone Response*)

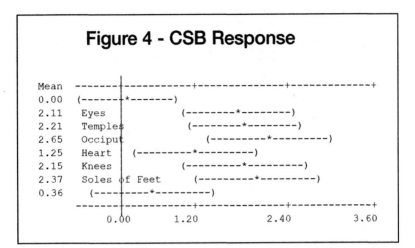

Figure 4 - CSB Response

```
Mean    -------+-----------+---------------+-------------+
0.00    (------+*-------)
2.11    Eyes                (--------*--------)
2.21    Temples             (--------*--------)
2.65    Occiput                 (---------*---------)
1.25    Heart   (---------*---------)
2.15    Knees               (---------*---------)
2.37    Soles of Feet           (---------*---------)
0.36    (----+----*---------)
        -------+-----------+---------------+-------------+
          0.00        1.20            2.40          3.60
```

Again we can observe in the illustration above (*Figure 4 - Cardiac Sensitivity to Baroreflex Response*) the general increase in response until the heart centre where it drops continuing to rise again at the knees and the soles of the feet.We can see in three out of the four observations that the energy flows and has an effect on the physical body but is stopped at the heart. So what does this mean? Many different traditions believe that the heart chakra is the point of balance with the physical, mental, emotional and spiritual bodies. It is the point at which our emotional roots and family experiences are held, where we translate the experience of our ancestors emotionally and unconsciously imprint their experiences on to ourselves. As I discussed earlier in this section it is also the point at which the masculine and feminine ancestral lines find a point of balance and harmony and if there is no point of balance there between the two lines then we are detrimentally affected by that on all levels. So we could perhaps draw a conclusion from the above that healing, therapy or energy healing will not be as effective or effective at all unless the underlying root is resolved, the heart of the matter as it were. This has long been hypothesised by those who seek to work with individuals holistically, but it is interesting to see the measurable effects and perhaps the limits that can be reached if an individual is "passive" in their healing experience or chooses not to 'see' their situation as it really is. Perhaps also it would be of interest in the future to monitor the physiological responses of individuals as they actively participate in a healing session or therapy. It would be extremely useful to be able to monitor someone's responses before, during and after a session and continue to monitor them over a period of time.

Chapter 3

Understanding the Ancestral Patterns and Accepting them as they are: Family Orders & Constellations

At this point I really felt like I'd taken a huge jump forward in my understanding of ancestral patterns and how to work with them. It is often at times like these, when you think you've cracked it, that the universe decides to show you what it is really all about and that is exactly what happened next...

I decided out of the blue to attend a workshop on "Ritual and Resonance - Healing the Family" run by Jill Purce, a teacher that I had previously attended courses with on sound healing. Looking back I had no idea what the course was actually about or what would be happening, I just felt drawn to attend. It wasn't even a spur of the moment thing as it was down in the other end of the country and involved trains, planes and automobiles. The course turned out to be working ceremonially with the resonant fields of the family healing the patterns in order to restore order to them through resonance and the voice. It astounded me and felt like I'd found a missing piece of the jigsaw puzzle. There were about 15 of us there for the workshop and instead of explaining what we would actually be doing or why the workshop leader opted for a more experiential approach. In essence we were there to take part in a ceremony to honour our ancestors and the family line and to release the pain and burdens that we were carrying for them. In all honesty I don't know if I would have gone along if I had read the leaflet properly and knew what was in store. We started by chanting whilst moving round clockwise in a circle holding hands, having not done a lot of sound work at that point or communal hand holding for that matter, to say I was out of my comfort zone was an understatement. We all stopped and continued the chant with our eye closed ready for the first individual to be chosen to start the ceremony. I opened my eyes to find the workshop leader standing in front of me. Hello deep end, so this is what you look like...I stood in the centre of this group of strangers and the leader asked me "what is your pain?" Then the ritual started with me choosing representatives of the family members that influenced my childhood whilst growing up. I picked four people to represent my Mother, Father, Grandfather and Grandmother. Then in turn I spoke to each of the family members with the purpose of acknowledging the hardships, challenges and difficulties they had experienced in their lives. I then arranged my family around by placing them according to how I felt they were connected to me. A spatial representation of our family bonds if you like. At this point the workshop leader started to question each of the representatives with regards to how they were feeling in the position that they had been placed: did they feel physically comfortable; how they felt emotionally; did they feel drawn to or repelled by another person in the family. Amazingly these strangers "tuned in" to my family members characteristics and soon the information began pouring in about relationships between family members, family members that I hadn't brought in but that were needed by the others to bring balance and resolution. As the other family members were introduced into the field the root of the feelings that I had been experiencing at the start of the ritual became quite obvious as the ancestral and family patterns emerged. This all took around an hour to take place but the effects of it rippled changes through my life for months afterwards as things started to change for me physically, emotionally, spiritually on any level you could think of. Within three months I had renewed ties with family members, broken my relationship with someone I had expected to marry, given up my career as a physicist and truly felt reconnected to who I was again. It was quite remarkable and fuelled my desire to find out more and understand how these ancestral patterns could be cleared once they were identified.The workshop itself was a derivation of "Family Constellation Systems" created by Bert Hellinger. Bert Hellinger is considered by many to be Europe's most innovative and provocative psychotherapists; he studied psychoanalysis, and eventually developed an interest in Gestalt Therapy and Transactional Analysis. It was in Hellinger's later training in family therapy that he first encountered the family constellations that have become the hallmark of his work. The ritual and ceremonial approach to the work is not traditional "Hellinger" style but was effecting and moving nonetheless.

Bert Hellinger's Family Constellation therapy is based on the principle that everyone within a family (the family system) is energetically connected within this family field by something that he calls the in-forming field. In his earlier work he proposed that in general there are two possible constellations that an individual can work with, either the family of origin that you have grown up with, or the present family which includes partners and children. When doing the constellation in a group setting the individual will choose representatives from the group for each of the family members (some constellation leaders opt for the individual to choose a representative for themselves also so that they can observe the full picture of their constellation). The individual then places the representatives in position to one another as a spatial representation of their emotional connection. The representatives are then asked to take note of how they are feeling emotionally, physically and how they respond to the other representatives. The leader then moves the representatives, with continual feedback from them, searching for where the tension is held and where the point of resolution is. Again generally speaking when working with the family of origin there can be an overwhelming array of connections and entanglements between family members that is drawing energy away from the family field, it is important to hold focus on the most powerful of those and to bring that in to balance for the individual concerned. With the present family the focus is very much on giving former partners their place, easing the relationship between the two masculine and feminine roles and the children involved. Ultimately we are looking for the point of balance that is comfortable for all the representatives and the individual in question. Hellinger's work continues to move forward and make new discoveries all the time. I have recently come back from one of his training camps where he shared his new method for working with constellations in large groups. It involves working with constellations without actively directing them and was simply incredible to watch and a great privilege to learn from him. One aspect of Hellinger's constellation work which some have difficultly coming to terms with is the phenomenological aspect of the informing field. How does the constellation leader 'link in' to the constellation and gain an understanding of the patterns at work there? How do the representatives of the family members connect with this person they are representing and intuit their emotions, thoughts and physical reactions so accurately? Well if you think about it we go back to the very ideas that we initially discussed those of a collective consciousness and an inherent link to those in our family and ancestral lines. If we accept that events or actions in a family can have an effect that travels down through the generations energetically then it is hardly a great stretch of the imagination to accept that in recreating a family field the representative family members will intuit the energy of that field and act accordingly. The new method that Hellinger has adopted for his work illustrates the effect of the family field very poignantly. He describes the new work as a 'multi-dimensional approach' that utilises the movements of the 'spirit-mind'. In true Hellinger style he started the seminar with an example without explaining anything before hand. An individual had come forward with a relationship issue; he was placed opposite a representative for his partner and then 20 randomly selected representatives were placed in a circle around the couple. The 20 represented the people that were influent upon the couple; they were then directed to go with their 'spirit-mind' as they felt moved, to trust and go with these movements and feelings. Over the course of the next hour the ancestral patterns gradually emerged and were unravelled in front of our eyes. At the time it reminded me of reading a Tarot spread with people instead of cards as the different individuals found their places within the family field. It was at times a little unsettling to watch but also fascinating. Interestingly in this particular constellation the majority of the representatives were dead but they had an influence on the couple as though they were alive. It was obvious from what we observed that until the dead have been given their place within the family field then they don't act as if they are truly dead, they still have an influence and are not at peace.

Working in this way with the 'spirit-mind' and following the movements of the soul allowed us to effectively communicate with the realms of the dead and to reconcile what had become separated and to acknowledge and honour the past in order to be free in the present. It was incredible to watch the 'spirit-mind' or the 'family-field' or the 'family-soul' take over and tell the story for the two individuals, at times when I was watching I wondered if it would ever come to a point of balance and resolution. I wondered at what point Hellinger would step in and take over. Of course he didn't need to; trusting the process and allowing the individuals their full time that they needed allowed the family to reach the point of resolution. At the end all within the family, those in the realms of the living and those in the realms of the dead, were at peace. Hellinger's approach encompasses the essential elements of the present family or the impact of the previous generation on the family of origin. He believes that going further and further back simply uncovers more and more entanglements that distract and dilute the energy. It then becomes easier and tempting to focus on the entanglements and become a victim of them instead of focusing on resolution and balance. This new approach of working with the 'spirit-mind' allows the deep events from the past to be uncovered, acknowledged and healed without necessarily knowing all the details and ins and outs of what happened.This is something I do wholeheartedly agree with; when working with someone I find that I see their family lines unfolding behind them likes swirls of smoke and I often see the break or the 'knot' in the line that is taking the energy. Very often this is something that has happened generations before and has been perpetuated and strengthened by more recent events within the family or in that particular aspect of the family line. It is important for the event or action to be acknowledged as the root cause (often this is done through a constellation) though it is unnecessary and somewhat dangerous to linger on the 'ins and outs', very often it is more comfortable to view our patterns of behaviour and choices from a distance and it is easier to avoid dealing with what we need to clear if it is something that is viewed to only be connected to the past. I am personally of the belief that when deep ancestral issues or perhaps even past life issues come to light it is a symptom of denial about the present circumstances. In saying this I am not belittling past life experience or deep ancestral influences, they certainly have their place but it is how they relate to you in the present moment that is the key. Very often they will hold symbolic information that must be seen with an honest eye. Constellations do not need to take place in a group setting; the energy and possibilities that are present within large groups are certainly advantageous but smaller groups and individual constellations are also very powerful and effective.An individual constellation is very useful for someone who is uncomfortable with group working, especially if the issue is particularly sensitive or if there is a very specific issue that the client wants to work with. When working with an individual it is possible to carry out the constellation either in their mind's eye through a series of guided visualisation exercises or through using representatives of the family members. For individual work I use pieces of paper or felt squares for the representatives which are placed in the family field, then by standing on each of the squares in turn I can begin to tune in to the field and we progress through the constellation together.It is important to remember that a family constellation is not a miracle cure for all. It can and does have incredible results for people however the responsibility for moving forward is always with the individuals themselves. Sophie Hellinger (Bert Hellinger's wife) describes the constellation as giving a "new picture" for the individual or the family but emphasises that the new picture has to be accepted in to the heart otherwise that old movie of past events, actions and results will just keep playing on repeat in your mind and experiences. It is easy to sense when there is unwillingness on the client's behalf to see the situation as it really is or to accept the changes or their own role. At this point the constellation has to be stopped until such time that the individuals are ready to move forward themselves. It is essentially in their hands. The fundamental basis of Hellinger's work and working with ancestral patterns in general, is to acknowledge and see "what is" as opposed to imagining what is and rejecting reality. As I mentioned previously it is perhaps more comfortable to think of our ancestors as something very far away and out of reach that lay dormant until we choose to think of them. However we know this now not to be the case, when the realm of the dead is not at peace then it is influent upon the realm of the living. By acknowledging, honouring and thanking our ancestors, by giving them a place in our hearts we can begin to move forward. But where should we begin? With our parents of course, they are the start of our ancestral line and thus for many the relationship with their parents is the stumbling block or the root of the issue that holds them back in their life. Hellinger likens the Mother in some ways to be representative of the "spirit-mind" and therefore a rejection of the Mother or indeed the Father is indeed a rejection of life itself. To say that you want different parents, that they weren't good enough, and that you didn't receive enough from them is to say that you want a different life; your life isn't good enough it is not enough for you. You cannot however change your parents, they are who they are, they are the only parents for you therefore they are the best parents for you. If this can be acknowledged with love then the individual become free with nothing to hold them back in life, if they cannot acknowledge or accept it as it is then they continue to perpetuate the same patterns within their life and pass them on to their own children. Their children will treat them as they treated their own parents.

Obviously this is presented here is a very simplistic fashion without any other dynamics that may be present in an individual's life but this does not take away from the profound effect of acknowledging, honouring and simply thanking the parents. For some the revelation of the sacrifices and energy required to be a parent cannot be fully comprehended until they themselves become a parent. I know myself that the birth of my son completely changed my life and I now look to my parents with new eyes and a new heart. In Hellinger's words the deepest enlightenment or revelation that can be experienced is to have a child and it comes at great cost to the parent and also to the child. You will notice that those that purport to seek enlightenment or claim to be on a spiritual path often separate from others to seek out their path to enlightenment in effect they are rejecting their family/their partner/their life and seeking out another.The things that have happened in the family in the past cannot be changed but they can be accepted in order to move on and the Ancestors can be acknowledged and allowed to rest in peace. This will allow us in turn to move forward with peace in our heart.

Exercise:

Before we move forward take some time to think about your own life. Write down any areas of your life that you feel blocked in or that cause you pain; be as honest with yourself as you possibly can. After you have done that write down the members of your immediate family that you grew up with and underneath their names write a brief history of their life, noting any major events or traumas.

Chapter 4

Patterns of Life: The Tarot

My first observations of the inherent patterns influencing the direction of our lives came from the world of the Tarot. The Tarot, best known as a divinatory tool dating from the 14th century, is my first love and continuing passion. The Tarot and the history of the Tarot is entrenched and animated with family, ancestral and archetypal patterns way back to its very roots. Until the last decade or so the history of Tarot has been one that has been pleasantly enshrined in the stuff of legend and myth but now most historians agree that Tarot cards appeared sometime in the mid to late 1400's in Italy, not long after regular playing cards were introduced to Europe in the 14th Century. The four suits were Swords, Wands (the Mamluk decks used polo sticks), Coins, and Cups. Each suit had ten pip cards and three 'court cards', a King, Knight, and Page, creating a 52-card deck. While that basic Italian suit system continued to be used, variations started to spring up in Spain and Germany. In some regular Italian-suited decks of the period, Queens had been added to the suit cards, creating a 56-card deck, and such a deck was the basis for Tarot. The subjects illustrated on Tarot's trump cards, now known as the Major Arcana, were also well-known before the 15th century, some them dating back to classical times with the fables of Love, Death, the Wheel of Fortune, the three Moral Virtues (justice, strength and temperance), and theosophical representations from Christian mythology (judgement). These were all present in the art of the time and still have a strong archetypal significance today. Generally the Tarot deck consisted of a regular 56-card deck, with a hierarchy of 22 archetypal trump cards. Creating the standard 78-card Tarot deck, originally referred to as carte da trionfi, cards with trumps and the majority of all Tarot decks in the 15th through 17th centuries share this same design. It is suggested that Tarot cards were produced as a game to amuse members of the Visconti, d'Este and other royal houses of Northern Italy with the members of the royal houses and political parties of the time portrayed within the archetypal images of the Major Arcana. A common 'myth' that has perpetuated is that the Visconti deck (67 of which are now held in Yale University's Cary Collection of playing cards) was created as a wedding gift with the bride portrayed as the 'Star, and the happy couple together in 'The Lovers'.The Tarot underwent another revolution in the early 1900s when occultism and esoteric studies were at the forefront of society again and no discussion on the origins and roots of Tarot would be complete without at least a mention of the Ryder-Waite Deck. Arthur Edward Waite, a Christian mystic, scholar of the occult and member of the Hermetic Order of the Golden Dawn interpreted the Major and Minor Arcana according to his own preferred mystical philosophy and that of the Golden Dawn. He really did revolutionise the deck with the artist Pamela Coleman-Smith and together they developed pictorial representations of the Minor Arcana suits which until that time had been represented by a series of geometrical patterns and shapes according to the particular suit. The pair also reordered the Major Arcana transposing the number cards 9 and 11 (Strength and Justice) to suit their magical workings with the Order of the Golden Dawn. Today the Tarot is widely accepted by many New Age enthusiasts, neo-Pagans, and psychics, as well as those who are interested purely in the study of the cards. Interestingly they have even been used by some psychologists within a therapeutic context and I have personally taught a psychologist to work with the Tarot for just this purpose. The present day interpretation of the Tarot now has some influence from Jungian psychology, early occult and esoteric theory but mainly from AE Waite. The vast range of Tarot decks available today, with themes ranging from

Celtic myths to Native American teachings is further proof of the Tarot's ability to bridge cultural divides and expose the core of all life experience as essentially touching on the same universal themes. It is now quite popular to set aside the traditional associations in favour of an intuitive interpretation of the cards where you are in effect tapping into universal archetypes from the unconscious mind. However to work with the archetypal symbolism inherent within the Tarot and alongside the mysticism hypothesised by AE Waite and others leads to a deeper understanding of the systems and patterns inherent within the Tarot and how the patterns are present within the cycle of your own life, where the patterns are rooted and perhaps how to move on from them.When it is used to its full capacity as a spiritual and divinatory system the Tarot can be an amazing tool for enlightenment, transformation and change. I first starting working with the Tarot system as a young teenager and went on to read professionally a couple of years later and continued for the next 15 years. It became an integral part of my life even when the focus of my days shifted in to more logical and scientific realms as I studied Physics at University. As I continued to work with individuals I would see the patterns affecting them in the present moment unfold in front of me in the cards. Tracing the pattern of behaviour back to its root gave the client some awareness of how they could stop the cycle, if they chose to, and move forward with their lives. The very nature of Tarot has a tendency to attract individuals in emotional crisis looking for answers and often looking for the responsibility of decision making in their life to be passed on to someone else. I found that using the Tarot to trace their own personal patterns instead of the base and crude application of fortune telling enabled the individuals to see the choices they had in front of them and to leave with an understanding of why certain things were occurring in their life.

Tarot is first and foremost a tool for self-awareness and self-empowerment, allowing observation of yourself, your life, your strengths and those areas causing you difficulty. Identifying the patterns and underlying trends from your past and present can highlight ways in which you can break out of those patterns which do not serve you anymore. Simply to recognise that you are following a pattern of behaviour can be pivotal. The Tarot is a gateway to our subconscious, where we store away our hopes and fears, our memories and our true self. All our problems and blockages in life are rooted within our subconscious. By tapping into it, through the use of Tarot, we can find solutions and seek guidance. When you lay out a spread of cards, the unique story of a life appears before you in picture form, with its own individual patterns made up of universal experiences and emotions, a powerful tool for understanding and influencing a life's pattern.There are traditionally 78 cards in a Tarot deck and within the 78 cards there are 56 Minor Arcana cards and 22 Major Arcana cards. 'Arcana' is the plural of the Latin word, Arcanum, meaning 'secret'. Over the years that I have been working with the tarot I have developed my own way of interpreting the cards that follows closely the theories of AE Waite but also encompasses the idea of ancestral knowledge and ancestral working. It is my personal preference to think of the system of Tarot as having three interlinked aspect of the Major Arcana, the Minor Arcana and the Court Families. No one aspect is more important than another as they are so interlinked and intertwined. I also like to think of the Tarot in terms of the symbolism of the spiral. The spiral is undoubtedly the oldest symbol of human spirituality. It has been found on every continent in the world scratched into rocks, burial tombs and sacred sites as well as the many naturally occurring examples in nature (think of snail shells, hurricanes, fern shoots etc). It is suggestive of a cycle of rebirth or resurrection. As well as being an ancient symbol of the goddess, the womb, fertility and the evolution of the universe. So how does it fit with Tarot? A popular teaching method for Tarot is to lay the entire 78 cards out on a circle, representing the circle of life, working through the Minor Arcana (with Court cards) and then the Major Arcana. This would suggest though that the Tarot (and the journey through life it is representing) comes back to the same point and is static which we know is really not true. I prefer to think in terms of the spiral where once you reach the end of the cycle that you are on, you continue onwards (or regress backwards) on your path taking with you the knowledge and experience as you continue. I also prefer to journey through the Tarot, for teaching and development purposes, starting with the Minor Arcana (through the suits of Wands, Swords, Cups and Pentacles), then in to the transitional and archetypal themes of the 22 cards of the Major Arcana, finishing with the Court Families of the four suits. I have very specific reasons for this. This chapter is not intended to be a 'How to' guide to working with Tarot, instead I hope to offer insights in to the world of Tarot and introduce it to you as a useful tool for exploring the archetypal and personal patterns that are imprinted in each of our lives. A gateway to the psychological and transpersonal aspects of the self, which can often at times be left to the realm or the psychologists and psychotherapists. When you can uncover and discover the patterns inherent within your own life and also see the broader, far reaching effects of the current situation you are in you take yourself closer to a point of resolution.On the surface, the Minor Arcana may appear to deal with mundane everyday issues but scratch the surface and they are a gateway to your psychological, spiritual and physical realities. They offer guidance on our chosen path, showing us the patterns at play within our lives and point towards their origin, mapping out the entanglements. They animate the patterns and allow them to come to life. I am not going to include an in depth discussion on their themes as that would be another book in and of itself, instead I shall highlight the patterns inherent to the Major Arcana and court families and illustrate the blueprint to the patterns of life that they hold within.Where the Minor Arcana is concerned with animating everyday life; the Major Arcana deals with traditional archetypes, universal influences and our family roots. These cards shed light on our spiritual and ancestral journey and illustrate turning points in our life, events that will happen or have happened that change our lives. Our attitude to these changes and phases in our life is the key. The situation and changes can work to our advantage or disadvantage depending on our outlook and what we are willing to acknowledge. I see the Major Arcana as having three distinct aspects or realms (the realm of the family, the ancestors and the dead) within the spiral with the Fool card acting as our guide through each aspect. I have provided some description on particular Major cards, but this is just a very basic start. The Fool is the naive and innocent child and can be placed anywhere within the Major Arcana as he acts as a guide; think of him as walking you through your family lines. The Fool stands at the start of the journey and represents infinite possibilities and infinite potentials viewing life through the eyes of your inner self, sometimes the inner child.

The Realm of the Family

The first aspect of the Major Arcana spiral is made up of the first seven numbered cards from The Magician through to the Chariot. It is the aspect that is concerned with who we are in the present situation and the influence our family and ancestry is having on us in the immediate moment. It is mainly concerned with personal emotional communication and interaction with others as we create bonds and forge ties with those around us.The first two cards are the Magician and the High Priestess, they act as gatekeepers to the masculine and feminine ancestral lines. The High Priestess & the Magician belong together they represent masculine and feminine duality of inner power. Whilst the Magician is more representative of being active in the material world the High Priestess is much more passive. She represents hidden knowledge from the ancestors, intuition and the unconscious mind. A balance between the Magician's control and the High Priestess's passivity is needed.The next two cards are the representatives of our parents and are the Empress and the Emperor. It is our relationship with the Empress and the Emperor (our Mother and Father) that determines our journey through the rest of the Major Arcana spiral and indeed through the spiral of our own life. Should we choose to distance ourselves and disassociate from them, then we find the transitions through the spiral much harder. When we reach the Hierophant and we do not have the support of the Mother and Father, or if we have rejected them, then we find ourselves blocked and unable to move. The influence or lack thereof becomes even more telling as we move in to the realm of the Lovers with the patterns laid in place for how we communicate emotionally with those around us. When we come to the Chariot we have the choice to take control, accept our roots and move forward or to flee further from whom we are as we seek out another path.The rejection of the parents in some form or another is at the root of many individuals' personal issues. By holding on to the belief that your parents weren't good enough, weren't there for you enough or by wishing that you had a different Mother or Father you are in effect rejecting or belittling your own life by rejecting and belittling them. In saying this I am not suggesting that hardships or trauma experienced as a child are justifiable or insignificant I am saying simply that there is a choice about the future. An acceptance that your Mother/Father is the only Mother/Father for you, that they gifted you your life in spite of what is cost both them and you and an acknowledgement of their place as your Mother/Father and your place as their child is far more freeing than holding on to the energy of the past and any mistakes that might have been made. To say "I wanted more" or "they weren't good enough" or "I reject you as my Mother/Father" is in effect rejecting your own life and creates a very difficult path forward for your life.

The Realm of the Ancestors

The next phase of the Major Arcana is represented by the next seven numbered cards from Strength to Temperance and is the aspect that brings up the patterns from the family generations that influenced your formative years. This aspect really highlights the struggle to come to terms with your place in your family system. The first two cards in this realm are Strength and The Hermit and they represent the changing relationship between parent and child as the child (or the individual looking back on their childhood). When the child is able to accept their parents as they are then they move forward to a place of strength and inner knowing. Strength in particular is a need to confront and release feelings and desires that have been locked away. It is indicative of a period of self-development with an honest appraisal of you and those around you.If however there is a rejection of the parents then the "child" sets off on a journey or path looking for what is missing (namely the relationship with the parent!) this journey is often at the sacrifice of their own family/personal relationship and it that instance The Hermit becomes a very self-serving place to be. This is because the energy of the Hermit highlights a need for a period of withdrawal to assess the family system and how you feel about it. The hermit and the lamp he holds represent inner wisdom, inner guidance and knowledge from the ancestors. Lingering too long in the indulgence of the Strength and Hermit can lead to events in life taking over as the patterns and fates from the past come to the fore to be repeated or to re-present themselves again. It is how these events are handled that is the key. If the family support and openness is there with the positive acceptance of the Child aspect then The Wheel of Fortune and Justice are a simple transition if however there is still rejection of the family and parental roots, the ancestral lineage, then they are indicative of a difficult period of 'why me?' type thinking.The Wheel of Fortune is based on the ancient belief that our fortunes change in a cyclic manner and embodies the mythology of 'The three fates' one who spins the thread of life, one who measures the length and one who cuts the length for each individual's life. The wheel represents the mysteries of fate, also embodies the laws of karma and ancestral knowledge. Justice indicates a lesson that has to be learned. Looking *honestly* at where you are, do you deserve to be here? Did your actions lead to this? What can you learn from those that have gone before you? What needs to be honoured and acknowledged or allowed to lie at rest? Again, the period represented by the next three cards within the cycle is either extremely freeing as the individual sees and accepts their place within their family system in respect to the entanglements that are present within both their Mother and Father's family lines, or extremely self-indulgent as the individual further disconnects from their roots and goes off on various personal/spiritual quests to find themselves. This behaviour is especially evident in The Hanged Man where from one angle the hanged man is suspended in space, viewed upside down he is quite happily dancing. He epitomises the martyr who blindly carries the burden of the fates that have gone before or the sacrifice of the self for the sake of the victims in the realm of the dead, which is often unwarranted and unwelcome. The Death card often symbolises a need to shed and let go of old patterns and if these patterns are held on to in can lead to physical/emotional illnesses. Signifying a time of change, coming to the end of a cycle and a need to let go of what was in order to move on. This can be a painful process if there is a fear of change and letting go with the temptation to stick to old habits where the individual can often have an inflated sense of self-importance as they place themselves within the centre of their family patterns. Temperance however heralds a sense of peace and freedom with a blessing from the ancestors in the realm of the dead to the realm of the living and also indicates the point of balance and resolution between the male and female ancestral lines. The word 'temperance' is derived from the Latin word 'temperare' which means 'to mix' or 'combine properly'. This card represents the ability to combine all parts of the self to be true and accepting of who you really are and where your place truly lies.

The Realm of the Dead

The final aspect of the Major Arcana uncovers some of the deeper ancestral patterns that have been passed down through the generations that become an inherent part of who we are. It can be more difficult to release and clear the energy associated with this aspect of the Major Arcana as the patterns are often old or entrenched. The ancestral energy that is influent from the Realm of the Dead is from those ancestors that are not at peace, who have been excluded or who have not been acknowledged. Of course those that we refuse to let go of and be at peace also influence from this realm, both in the symbolic world of the Tarot as well as our own reality. It is represented by the final seven numerical cards of the Major Arcana, from the Devil through to the World. The quests started in the family and ancestral realms of the Major Arcana can often involve intense but one-sided relationships with other individuals that are similarly disconnected from their family, this is highlighted by the ancestral aspect of the cycle in particular with The Devil and The Tower. The Devil especially highlights the self-destructive patterns of addictive behaviours such as alcoholism, drug and even food addiction. These addictions again link back to the rejection of the parental influences of the Empress and the Emperor and reflect the communication issues of the Lovers although the patterns held may be older than the current or previous generation. The Devil links back to the lovers with the theme of choices and shows an individual feeling trapped in a situation but unwilling to make the choice to change. The card can also indicate that the individual is letting their desires overpower their judgment and that they are not basing their decisions on the full facts. There is a need here to break free from a negative situation or negative behaviour pattern that really belongs to another. Again as mentioned previously the theme of the Devil is strongly linked to addictions and substance abuse. This in effect is a long-term suicide bid and often is because someone in missing from the family field. In most cases it is the Father that is missing or a member of the male line and this links back in with the first aspect or realm of the family and the relationship with the Emperor and the Hierophant. The link to the Lovers and emotional communication can result in very destructive relationship patterns as women with alcoholism in the male line of their family become entangled in relationship with a similar destructive masculine element. The Tower represents difficult experiences and violent upheaval that is repeated throughout the family lines. Occurrences of abuse, suicide, violence as well as fertility/birth issues are very often the hallmarks of this type of ancestral pattern that is left unchecked. Often arises when a family has attempted to erase the past by moving away from their roots, in most cases the energy of the past will still worm its way back in to future generations regardless of the location as one or more of the descendants resonates and unconsciously seeks to absolve the past.

We loop back and have a chance to revisit our roots and essentially 'come home', take our place and accept our true fate with the final phase of the aspect or realm of the dead as we have another opportunity to reintegrate in to our place as see with honest eyes where our place is... This is possible with the peace, healing and recovery of the Star, an acknowledgement of the mysteries of the family system or of that which has been hidden with the Moon and aided by the freedom, letting go and liberation of the Sun. After the night comes the dawn and this card represents strong success and break through with support from the ancestors on your journey. Judgement is associated with Karmic balance, you will reap what you have sown, indicative of acting responsibly and acknowledging your place as well as whom and what have gone before you. We finish with the World, you are in your place, you are self-aware and life is harmonious and balanced. Pause, enjoy what you have accomplished, then continue the spiral of life.

The Court Families

This brings us on to the Court Families. In my opinion the Court Families are the people that have journeyed through the spiral of life and have the scars to prove it. They carry with them the knowledge of the element of their particular suit as well as the archetypal knowledge of the Major Arcana. They represent you, your family members and your ancestors and when you connect to them they become you, your family members and ancestors and tell the tales of your life, your family life and the patterns therein. They can show you how these patterns are being acted out by the people surrounding you and the different situations occurring in your life. The four suits of the Minor Arcana (Wands, Swords, Cups and Pentacles) all have elemental associations which represent the essence of the suit and its purpose. We start with the suit of Pentacles. It is concerned with the physical world, our ancestral line, our family and our place in it. The function of this suit is to help us to ground ourselves in order to progress and literally "find our feet" in who we are and where we come from. We then move on to the suit of swords which is the element of air. Swords have the reputation, unjustifiably of being very negative. They can signify pain, anger and destruction however being the element of air is very often the perception of something rather than a physical reality. They signify a need to cut through illusion and pain. Their main function is to give clarity on where we are in the present moment, to show us any patterns or blocks and what needs to be done to clear them so we can move on and heal. So, in essence they highlight the burdens or fates from the ancestors that we are carrying forward.Next is the suit of cups. Cups are related to the element of water which is concerned with emotion and emotional communication, connections with others and our intuitive sense of self. The Cups indicate and suggest where the healing of the past karma needs to occur. They also link in to the female ancestral line.The suit of Wands relates to the element of fire, which embodies connection to spirit, transformation, change, clearing, and the drive to move forward. The Wands also provide a connection to the male ancestral line.They each bring different messages:

- Messages of karmic influences with ancestral rooting in the earthy pentacles to the **male ancestral** line
- Messages of clarity of where you are now with the air suit of swords to the **female ancestral** line
- Knowledge of how to heal past karma with the watery cups to the **female ancestral** line
- The energy of transformation with the fire and the wands to the **male ancestral** line

Below is a guide to the Court Families, with their masculine and feminine aspects. The feminine line is carried by the Page (Princess in some decks) and the Queen; the masculine line is carried by the Knight and the King.

The Wand Family

The Wand Family helps us to understand where we are being blocked, where change needs to occur and what needs to be cleared through their element of Fire with strong male ancestral energy.

The Female Line

The female line of the Wand family in youth is not rooted; there is a need to look to the other siblings, or for missing siblings within the family in order to help her find her place. She quickly loses interest and moves on amassing a pile of unfinished tasks and relationships. The older female Wand, with the patterns left unchecked, will have amassed many responsibilities through her inability to say no to her passions. She is open to emotional blackmail and her interaction with the male line is often destructive upon her, she is ruled by her passion and guilt. It would be wise to look to the former partners of this lady to see the path that lies behind her.

The Male Line

The young male Wand has an unquenchable desire to prove himself to family and those close to him often losing sight of why he has started something. He seeks to be seen and is often overlooked. As he grows older he becomes strong minded, dominating and assertive and often appears as a 'block' for individuals to overcome as he has little awareness of others on their own path as he expects everyone else to follow him to the fates that he himself is bound to follow.

The Sword Family

The Sword family brings us the honest clarity of where we are in the present and what influences or patterns from the past are affecting us in the present. They show us, in their own particular style, what we need to cut from our lives or what thought patterns we need to release. There is strong female ancestral energy with the Swords.

The Female Line

The young female Sword is hesitant to put herself back out there and have the same pattern repeat itself (this can be a perception rather than a learned behaviour as she strongly carries the ancestral line). Guarded and detached in emotional relationships and communication,she can seem cold to outsiders.

The sense of detachment continues as she grows older, she is excellent at seeing others as they really other but cannot apply this emotional logic to herself. She feels isolated from her masculine counterparts.

The Male Line

In youth he is completely reactionary. Everything is in his head and is intellectualised and he finds emotional communication uncomfortable. He is constantly on the defensive as he is not rooted in who he is, he feels trapped between the masculine and feminine lines. With age he becomes calm, calculating with a tendency for narrow-mindedness. He 'remembers' the burdens from the past and carries them with him unconsciously which leads him to detach. He finds emotional communication difficult and feels disconnected from the influence of the Feminine line. He often has a string of broken relationships behind him to match with the Queen of Wands. His detachment leads him to feel little for others though he can appear very charming.

The Cup Family

The Cup Family carries the knowledge of how and where to heal Karma from the past down the lines and also strongly carries the energy of the female ancestors.

The Female line

In youth the female cup is ruled by her emotions and intuition and holds on to other people's emotions like a sponge. She has the energy of being stuck between the family lines but feels extreme loyalty to the female line as there is often a pattern of trauma perpetuated by the masculine line. As she ages is still ruled by emotion but instead of focusing on her own emotions (like the page) she finds it more comfortable to work with other people's emotions in order to move them forward, staying firmly stuck herself. She has an intuitive knowledge of past karma but refuses to acknowledge or clear her own. Here you will find many a social worker, carer or therapist unconsciously trying to free themselves by helping others.

Male Line

So obsessed is the young male with his own emotions and his own perfection that he is oblivious to others. Is constantly trying to live up to an ideal that he has set for himself (in reality it has been set before him in his family line but he has no awareness of this). He grows up with far more awareness and guilt. He is linked more to his family's feminine line than the masculine and feels unexplained guilt because of this; he will put family and responsibility to family before himself and is often mistreated within this role.

The Pentacle Family

The Pentacle family brings the karmic influences from our ancestral rooting in to our physical reality as well as carrying a strong masculine link to the ancestors.

The Female Line

She is overly influenced by what is expected of her and has a tendency to veer towards the masculine line in the family and doesn't hold respect for the feminine line. She will shoulder the responsibility for old guilt and needs to release it. As she matures she can often find herself placed in a role as she carries forward the responsibilities that belong to others. She is the grown up version of the young page that hasn't realised that she is living her life for someone else. Often the Father or a significant member of the masculine line will be missing from the family system.

The Male Line

In youth he is someone who sticks to his path as he sees it and will take the road that is right for him even if it is the road less travelled. He is determined, strong-willed and sticks to his guns. He is unconsciously finishing what those before him have started and has a stronger family link with the older generations rather than his peers. He becomes a self made man from the school of hard knocks who strives to be a provider so that the past does not catch up with him. He often has no awareness of why he strives so hard and can lose sight of the family he has created himself as he is driven by the past. Releasing the past will free him from this, there is a positive relationship with the Mother but the Father is often detached (e.g. masculine line of the Sword family). It should be noted that the practice of divination and using the Tarot as a tool for working with individuals on their ancestral and family patterns requires a different approach to working with the spiral for your own development. The Tarot spiral is then used as a tool for the reader to place the individual within the spiral and to uncover the trends or patterns inherent in the present moment and to allow them to be traced back through the spiral to their root, thus offering the individual an opportunity to clear and move forward. You do not have to use the cards in the traditional manner for divination when you want to work for yourself. Accessing the energy of the Tarot through a visualisation meditation is a very effective way of highlighting some of the patterns that are currently at play in your own life. If you have a Tarot deck that you currently work with you may want to lay out the four Court Families and spend some time familiarising yourself with them for the next exercise. Do not worry if you do not have a Tarot deck you can still try to the following exercise. It would be useful to either read through the exercise a few times before you try it, to record it (leaving sufficient space for your own personal exploration) or to have a friend read it aloud for you. The family members that come to you during the exercise may be actual members of your own family or they may be symbolic representations.

Exercise for Connection to your own Court Families

1. It's probably best to be lying down for this meditation, make sure that you are comfortable and warm before you start. You

may need a blanket as your body temperature may drop when you are relaxed.

2. Close your eyes and relax down your body. Imagine water flowing over the front of your body washing away any tension or stress from your face your neck and chest, your legs, all washed away through the soles of your feet into the earth. Now imagine water flowing down over the back of your body, washing any tension and stress from the back of your head, your neck, your shoulders, back and legs. All this is washed into the earth through the soles of your feet. Now imagine water flowing through your crown chakra, flowing through your entire body, cleansing you of any stressful thoughts or emotions, taking away any stress and tension, all this flowing away through the soles of your feet leaving you completely relaxed.

3. Now visualise yourself lying down in the middle of a clearing. You are lying down on a blanket; the sun is shining and warming you. There is a light breeze ruffling the grass and trees surrounding your clearing. You are completely at peace.

4. Now it is time to invite in the Fool from the Major Arcana. He is going to be your guide for this journey. Notice how he looks, how he makes you feel. Spend some time connecting with his energy and listen to what he has to say.

5. Once you have connected with the Fool it is time to ask him to bring to you the members of the wand family who bring the element of Fire. Notice how they look, how they makes you feel. Spend some time connecting with their energy and listen to what they have to say. When you are ready ask them "What is my fear?" listen and feel the message they bring to you. Thank them and allow them to leave.

6. It is now time to ask the Fool to bring to you the members of the Sword family who bring the element of Air. Notice how they look, how they makes you feel. Spend some time connecting with their energy and listen to what they have to

say. When you are ready ask them "What do I need to release and let go of?" listen and feel the message they bring to you. Thank them and allow them to leave.

7. It is now time to ask the Fool to bring to you the members of the Cup family who bring the element of Water. Notice how they look, how they makes you feel. Spend some time connecting with their energy and listen to what they have to say. When you are ready ask them "What do I need to heal?" listen and feel the message they bring to you. When you feel ready thank them and allow them to move onwards.

8. It is now time to ask the Fool to bring to you the members of the Pentacle family forward who bring the element of Earth. Again notice how they look, how they makes you feel. Spend some time connecting with their energy and listen to what they have to say. When you are ready ask them "What is my purpose?" listen and feel the message they bring to you. Thank them and allow them to leave.

9. Spend some time again alone with the Fool, you can ask him if he has any further guidance for you. When you are ready gradually bring your awareness back to the room you are sitting in, become more aware of your physical body, wriggle your fingers and toes. When you are ready open up your eyes.

You may want to spend some time recording your experience so that you do not forget it, what seems vivid and unforgettable at the time does have a tendency to slip away and you will be doing further work with this experience.

Further work on your own Patterns

I have designed a simple nine-card spiral Tarot spread specifically for focusing on ancestral patterns which you can use for your own development. It is also an excellent tool if you are already familiar with the Tarot and would like to incorporate ancestral patterns in to your work with others. The layout is illustrated below *Figure 5 – Ancestors Spiral Spread.*

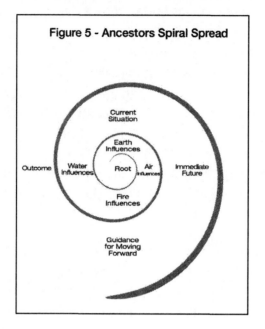

Figure 5 - Ancestors Spiral Spread

1. The Root Cause
2. Earth Influences – message from the Pentacle Family
3. Air Influences – message from the Sword Family
4. Fire Influences – message from the Wand family
5. Water Influences – message from the Cup Family
6. Current Situation
7. Immediate Future
8. Guidance for moving forward
9. Final Outcome

An example spread of an individual I worked with is given below (*Figure 6 - Ancestors Spiral Sample spread*). Karen had chosen to come because she felt that there was a destructive pattern affecting the masculine line within her family, she had been told that the family was cursed but didn't accept that was true and wanted some answers. From the spread you can see that the root cause of the issue has been highlighted by the Justice card from the Major Arcana indicating something that needs to be honoured, acknowledged and laid to rest, that coupled with the need to let go of the old patterns and acknowledge the ancestors and allow them to be at peace (highlighted by the Death card in the immediate future). The cards were in effect screaming of something that was being carried forward and perpetuated unnecessarily. The messages from the male aspects of the family spoke more of the burdens that the female.

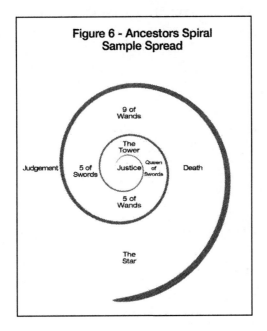

Figure 6 - Ancestors Spiral
Sample Spread

1. Justice   6. Nine of Wands
2. The Tower   7. Death
3. Queen of Swords   8. The Star
4. Five of Wands   9. Judgement
5. Five of Swords

When I discussed this with Karen it came to light that the reason the family felt uprooted was because the family had been uprooted two generations ago. Her great grandfather had murdered a family in the village they lived in; the male head of the family owed him money and in retribution he set their family home alight, the entire family perished including two infant sons. Instead of handing himself in he forced his own family to flee with him and never showed any remorse or acknowledgement of his actions. The pattern that was left affecting the family involved sudden traumatic death within the male line and bankruptcy. Quite a dramatic example but the karmic, ancestral parallels are very clear to the observer. By acknowledging the victims of her Great-Grandfather my client started to clear away some of the burden from her family line. However this is where the Tarot starts to fall down as a tool for working with the ancestors. Its strength lies in highlighting the areas of concern however when the pattern runs very deep a simple acknowledgement of what has gone before isn't always enough. At this point I started exploring other avenues.

Chapter 5

Ancestral Sounds: Beginning to Clear the Patterns

Blood of our Blood
hear our call
We stand as one,
before you all
We feel your presence,
strong and true
And forge the link,
from us to you
A sacred line,
that flows to ground
The line is unbroken,
the line is Sound. *

Working with Sound to Clear Blocked or Stagnant Energy within your Body through the recitation of prayers, chants and mantras is found in many different traditions from many different countries. There are also different traditional associations for the use of sound, in the Hindu, Buddhist, Christian, Islamic and Hebrew traditions, you will find the chanting of prayers or recitation of a divine name as part of spiritual practice. In shamanic, druidic or more pagan traditions, chanting, toning and mantra are used in ritual, ceremony and prayers with the purpose of invoking divine entities such as a God or Goddess, for healing, devotional work or perhaps magic. There has been much research and study in to the

---

*An invocation to the ancestors written by Nicola Mackay as part of a day of toning ceremony on a sound healing intensive with Jonathan Goldman in 2005.

use and efficacy of sound for healing. Dr. Herbert Benson (the Director Emeritus of the Benson-Henry Institute (BHI), the Mind/Body Medical Institute Associate Professor of Medicine, Harvard Medical School) pioneered research focusing on stress and the relaxation response in medicine. In his research, the mind and the body are one system; his research explores the use of meditation and chanting to reduce stress responses. He also defined the "relaxation response", which is a reduction of heartbeat , brain waves and respiration and observed this relaxation response in his research. In fact the research that has looked in to the effects of sound and sound healing on the human body and nervous system has found very similar if not identical results to those studies investigating the effects of energy healing on the physical body and nervous system.

Research has also shown that recitation of mantras has the effect of stimulating the acupuncture meridians inside the mouth and on the roof of the mouth increasing the flow of energy in the body (*Shannahoff-Khalsa, DS et al.* 1989). Interestingly, stimulating the same point in the roof of the mouth whilst simultaneously contracting the perineum is a technique that is used in Chinese Qi Gong practice to also increase the flow of energy within the body. It's also been found that chanting and toning with intention will affect the left and right hemispheres of the brain causing them to synchronise or shift into a different state. Other physiological effects include the release of the hormone melatonin, oxygenation of the brain, reduction in heart rate and blood pressure again stimulating the relaxation response that is observed in energy healing also (*Werntz, DA. Et al.* 1983)However you don't have to be chanting or working with sound directly to experience a healing effect (though the effect will be to a lesser degree). Dr. Alfred Tomatis in his amazing work has also found that listening to certain chants has a beneficial effect on the physical and subtle bodies too (*Tomatis, A. A.* 1991). He is probably most generally known for his work uncovering "The Mozart Effect" which has becoming popularly translated to mean that listening to Mozart will improve your mental agility (*Gilmore, Tim.* 1999). However he is a prolific researcher and scientist who is extremely interested in the effect of sound, he used recording of the sounds of Gregorian Monks to stimulate the ears, brain and nervous systems of his clients. He also discovered that sounds that are rich in vocal harmonics stimulate and have a positive effect on the brain and the nervous system. Taking this hypothesis to a commercial level we can perhaps see why certain types of music are utilised by certain companies at certain times; supermarkets and shopping malls are perhaps some cynical examples. He spent a lot of time working with autistic children attempting to enable them to recognise and respond to their mother's voice. He designed a system that attempted to simulate the sound of the mother's voice as it would be heard by the child in the womb and along with specially filtered classical music (which is where the Mozart Effect comes from) he would gradually work with the sounds and the child so that the child could begin to accept and respond to the Mother's real unfiltered voice. This method had tremendous results with children crying as they were able to recognise their mother's voice for the first time. It is also said of Tomatis' work that he believed that many issues such as learning disabilities, dyslexia, depression, schizophrenia, autism etc were caused by an initial trauma rooted in the family such as broken relationships and lack of communication about events or entanglements in the family. He sought the cooperation of the parents and grandparents in the treatment of individuals which is very interesting when we look at his work in the context of family and ancestral patterns.

Working with Chant and Mantra

There are specific mantras to balance and align the chakras as well as the physical and subtle bodies. The Bija/seed mantras from the Hindu system are an example of this. Another example can be found within the Reiki system, known as the Kotodama. The ancient Japanese believed that all things in the Universe are created from a primordial sound (U) which split into two opposing sounds (A) and (O). Kotodama literally translates as 'word spirit'. They feature in various aspects of Japanese culture, including Shintoism and Buddhism, and are used in martial arts such as Aikido. The ancient Japanese believed that words had power over things in nature; if you knew the right sound, you could control the elements themselves, for example female pearl divers used the word sound 'su' to calm the waters before they dived to collect their treasure. One of the Reiki symbols, Hon Sha Ze Sho Nen, known colloquially as the distant healing symbol can be used very effectively to clear energy related to your family and ancestral line.

The symbol is made up of Japanese characters or *kanji* and is

Figure 7 - Han Sha Ze Sho Nen

illustrated left in *Figure 7 – Hon Sha Ze Sho Nen*. The constituent characters can be found in a Japanese-English dictionary and translate literally as: "This (Hon) person (Sha) rightly (Ze) adjusts (Sho) thoughts/ feelings/ desires (Nen)". However, the symbols aren't written as the Japanese would normally write them, but have been overlapped (parts of each symbol are the same as parts of the next, so they have been combined). This has the effect of strengthening the symbolism and energy of the kanji, this is a technique found throughout many systems, from Chinese Buddhist and Taoist practices to bind-runes in the European/ Nordic traditions.In practical healing terms, the most common function of this symbol is to facilitate sending Reiki/energy over time and distance, so that you can channel healing to someone in another room, another house, or another country. However I also believe that the use of the sound representation of the HSZSN Kotodama can release karmic or ancestral energy that we are holding in our physical or energetic bodies by way of healing past hurt or lessening the impact of traumatic events, or paving the way for a positive outcome.

Using the HSZSN Kotodama

I use two versions of the Kotodama, one using the pure vowel sounds and the other the harder consonant sounds. The chanting of vowels has very similar benefits to mantric chanting. Vowel sounds are considered sacred in many different traditions, from the Hebrew Kaballah to Tibetan Buddhism. It is sometimes easier to focus on pure vowel sounds as we are not trying to interpret the meaning of the words that we are chanting as we are chanting. Vowels in particular have specific harmonics that affect both the physical and the etheric bodies.To use the Kotodama, prepare a quiet space for yourself and ensure that you are seated comfortably. Focus on your breath, breathing from deep within your belly. Then simply begin chanting from deep within, placing your hands on any areas you wish to channel healing to that you may have become aware of when you were scanning your body with the exercise in Chapter 2. Sound the kotodama on the out breath and for the full out breath.The soft vowel chant for the symbol is **oh-ah ay-oh-ay**. The hard consonant chant for the Masters symbol is **Ho-ah Zay Oh-nay**. You may want to spend some time in silence when you are finished; often it is within the absence of the sound that you will have the strongest experience of release. It would also be worthwhile to record some notes to look back on.

Working Compassionately - The 'Ah' Sound

The 'AH' sound is considered to be a very powerful mantra. It is a sacred seed syllable as well as a vowel sound. The vowels are considered to be divinely inspired and they are held sacred in many different traditions with the belief that the vowels belong to the realms of spirit and the harder consonant sounds belong to the physical realm of Earth. The 'AH' sound is also connected with generating compassion for the self and others.Most mystical traditions that use vowels sounds in association with the chakras use the 'AH' sound for sound of the heart chakra. As mentioned earlier this chakra, located in the centre of the chest is associated with love and compassion and our ability to feel unconditional love and compassion for others. It is also believed that the 'AH' sound is the sound that is produced by us on our first breath when we are born and the last sound we make as we exhale in to death.

Exercise:

1. It's probably best to be sitting down for this exercise, make sure that you are comfortable and warm before you start. You may need a blanket as your body temperature may drop when you are relaxed.

2. Spend a moment relaxing and focussing your awareness on your physical body. Allow your breath to flow naturally and quietly observe the sensations in your own body.

3. In your mind's eye see your Mother standing in front of you. As you see her see her family line stretch out behind her. See her connection and service to that line and also her entanglements to that line.

4. As you see all of that play out in your mind's eye take a moment to remind yourself that in spite of all the entanglements, all the other directions she was pulled in she was still able to be your Mother.

5. Bring your attention now to your heart centre, feel it opening towards your Mother.

6. Now simply begin to chant the 'AH' chant on each out breath

and feel your compassionate connection to your Mother.

7. Take some time to sit in the silence and to notice how you feel now.
8. You may wish to say something at this point to your Mother. Often simple is best, try saying "yes, mum" or "yes, _____" however you referred to your own Mother and "Thank you".

Now it is time to repeat the above exercise for your Father.

1. Spend a moment to centre yourself, relaxing and focussing your awareness on your physical body. Allow your breath to flow naturally and observe the sensations in your own body.
2. In your mind's eye see your Father now standing in front of you. As you see him see his family line stretching out behind him. See his connection and service to that line and also his entanglements to that line.
3. As you see all of that play out in your mind's eye, take a moment to remind yourself that in spite of all the entanglements, all the other directions he was pulled in he was still able to be your Father.
4. Bring your attention now to your heart centre, feel it opening towards your Father.
5. Now simply begin to chant the 'AH' chant on each out breath and feel your compassionate connection to your Father.
6. Take some time to sit in the silence and to notice how you feel now.
7. You may wish to say something at this point to your Father. Again simple is best, try saying "yes, dad" or "yes, _____" however you referred to your own Father and "Thank you".

Again, you may want to spend some time in silence when you are finished and to take some notes about your experience that you can read over later. Don't worry if you did not feel able to or wish to say something to either or both of your parents. If you found the exercise difficult it is worth working on again over a period of time. Remember the connection to blocked healing in Chapter 3? How the heart centre seems to have the ability to limit our ability to heal? Simply working with the "AH" chant and focusing on the heart centre whilst chanting will help to release some of the blocked energy and allow you to move forward in your emotional relationships.

Words that Heal in the Context of a Constellation

Sometimes during a constellation, or even in a one on one session with an individual looking in general at the ancestral patterns it becomes clear that there is a need to express outwardly what is being expressed inwardly. For example I was working with a young woman who was very depressed and was suffering from bouts of debilitating illnesses that could not be treated. I discovered that her Mother was battling cancer and had been for a couple of years. Inwardly the young woman was saying "I will go instead of you" when this is brought out in to the open it becomes much clearer and the individual can see the pattern of behaviour clearly and how the order within the family has been disrupted by this. We then worked together to free her from this pattern and she was able to say, "even though you are leaving, I will stay".When the orders in the family system become disrupted or 'out of kilter' in this way it is often hidden away and not easily recognised by those involved. Once it has been brought to light the family system can re-order itself and be brought back in to balance. When the truth of the situation is not only acknowledged but spoken aloud then the distorted views seems to simply fall away. Going back to the old traditions of 'soothsayers' it is believed that hearing the truth spoken has the power to sooth a tormented soul. There are many 'statements of power' or 'words that heal' that are used when working with the ancestors however they need to be used in the context of a particular situation to be effective. Examples of their use are illustrated in Chapter7.

Chapter 6

Working with the Ancestors in the Realm of the Dead: Family & Ancestral Sessions

The whole purpose and focus of working with your Ancestors and family lines is to allow you to reconnect with who you are, to take your place and to remember your place. By seeing and acknowledging who has gone before you can pave the way for those that will follow in your footsteps and importantly allow you to see it all as it really is. In discussing the different aspects and approaches to this type of work I am not favouring one over another, it is important to find the path of working that you connect with the most and is the most comfortable for you as an individual as you need to 'feel' and intuit your way back to your place.When I work with individuals now I use a combination of all the approaches that I have outlined in this book, changing and bending to suit each individual client. One thing is always constant in each session; I always start with the same question "Why are you here?" Some people laugh at this thinking I am being flippant, some are annoyed expecting me to know and to guide them to where they should go, some know me from my early days when I worked purely with intuition and the Tarot and become tight-lipped thinking I am hood-winking them in to giving me information. This is far from it, in asking why are you here? I am passing the responsibility for their decisions, their choices, their healing if you like, back to them. If they are fully present with me during a session and take responsibility to be present then the effects will be far greater than if I were to simply 'read' their energy and proclaim their place for them, they in turn can fully participate and don't have to defend against someone telling them how their life is. Again think back to the rejected energy of the heart chakra observed in the research and outlined in Chapter 2. Often that one very simple question can have surprising answers, when the individual is allowed a moment to sit with the question you can go from well I'm not sure why I'm here but I just felt I had to to something that is a stronger reflection of their inner self, their truth. Others start at a different extreme, they are there because of their partners behaviour, their Mother, their Father, their job etc again if they are given time to think about themselves their truth will come out also.Whilst they are either sitting pondering their truth or speaking it out loud, this reason that they are here, I am sitting opposite them connecting with their energy. Similar to the way in which I described in Chapter 2 for connecting with your own energy I sit with the person opposite and allow their energetic patterns, as I experience them, to appear before me. It becomes clear if the individual is giving an honest description of their situation or symptoms. When I say honest I do not mean that I am sensing whether or not someone is being deceitful (though this can happen) what I mean is that often the entanglements within the family can be very old or very deep in which case the individual may be confused as to what is actually going on.As I sit with them and connect with them and tune in to their family energy I start to explore the ancestral line. I see the lines unfolding behind them likes swirls of smoke; I often see the break or the "knot" in the line that is taking the energy. Sometimes I see the person connected with this or who the nearest person to them is who is perpetuating this pattern. This can be something that has happened generations before that has strengthened by more recent events within the family or in that particular aspect of the family line. It is important for the event or action to be acknowledged as the root cause (often this is done through a constellation) though it is unnecessary and somewhat dangerous to linger on the 'ins and outs', very often it is more comfortable to view our patterns of behaviour and choices from a distance and it is easier to avoid dealing with what we need to clear if it is something that is viewed to only be connected to the past. I then share my experiences with the client and at this point we will discuss relevant events from their family or the family of their partner. Often at this point the issue that they are choosing to work on will become clearer to them as well. When working with an individual it is possible to carry out the constellation either in their mind's eye through a series of guided visualisation exercises or through using representatives of the family members. For individual work I use pieces of paper or felt squares for the representatives. The squares are placed in the family field and by standing on each of the squares in turn I can begin to tune in to the field and we progress through the constellation together. I have illustrated below the basic flow of the constellations that I have observed in *Figure 8- Spiral Constellation and Realms of Influence*. The ancestral patterns generally follow the flow of the spiral, echoing the patterns observed with the Tarot. The spiral flows from the realm of the family, to the realm of the ancestors and then on to the realm of

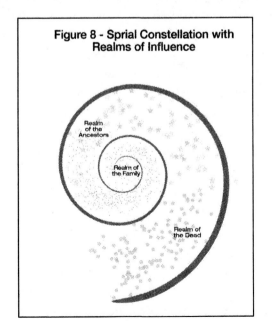

Figure 8 - Sprial Constellation with Realms of Influence

Realm of the Ancestors

Realm of the Family

Realm of the Dead

the dead. There is a difference between the realm of the ancestors and the realm of the dead, those that are within the realm of the ancestors are still influencing the living whether they are alive or not however those that reside in the realms of the dead are at peace (living family members who are pulled to the outer layers of the spiral i.e. the realms of the dead are attempting to follow the dead).

If the individual is particularly visual and open to guided visualisation then we will use constellations based within the realm of the imagination. This is particularly useful when dealing with events that have happened much further back in the ancestral line, again as I stated previously very deep events or events from many generations back can be easier to focus on for the individual initially if they are reluctant to see their present situation as it really is. By using the guided visualisation to clear the past we can then move forward to dealing with their more present relationships whether it is with Mother/Father or Partner/Child with an actual physical constellation. If an individual has difficulties with the imagined constellation or finds the experience too overwhelming them the patterns can easily be explored through the use of Tarot.We then work together to find the point of resolution and balance for the family and the ancestors, sound is incorporated in to the work either in the form of the 'words that heal' or chant exercises to release energy.At the end of the session after we have reached the point of resolution (or we have reached a point where we can go no further for the time being) I then talk the individual though a simple ritual or exercise for acknowledging further what we have uncovered that they can do in their own space to strengthen the work that we have done together and this new picture for the family that we have created. This further work can often include a simple acknowledgement ritual for family members that need to be brought back in to the family field as well as the individual's heart. This can involve a ritual of acknowledgement such as lighting a candle in someone's honour as you affirm out loud again that you give them a place in your heart. Planting a tree or evergreen plant/herb in the earth is a very positive way of acknowledging a child or sibling that has been lost or excluded (this is not of course limited to children/siblings) as it is giving life again and rooting the tree or plant (which becomes a representative for the missing individual) will firmly underline that the ancestor now has their place. The choice of tree/plant/herb can be picked appropriately as well as there are many different magical associations. One particular client that I worked with felt that the property she now owned and lived at was carrying a curse because of the string of negative happenings that had assailed her since moving there including the breakup of her marriage, failure of her business, loss of her job and the breakdown of every piece of electrical equipment or motor vehicle that came in to contact with the house or the land that is was built upon. We investigated the history of the property and found it to be the site of a clan battle centuries before. By working with the land, planting specific herbs and plants such as rosemary and sage and also burning willow to honour the dead that had sacrificed their life there we were able to clear the echoes of the past and the dead were able to rest at peace. When an individual is struggling with letting go of the past or accepting the situation they are in as it truly is, then some visualisation exercises where they imagine the ancestor/family member before them and allow themselves to feel the connection as it truly exists, is a useful way of paving the way for healing and further work. Again the responsibility always lies with the individual to take each step forward.

Chapter 7

Dipping your toe into the Realms of Influence

The following are some examples of ancestral and family sessions that I have carried out in individual sessions. I have not gone in to full detail or outlined every aspect of the session; instead I have offered some observations of the patterns uncovered and the resolutions that came to light. (The names of the individuals and some details of the sessions have been changed.) It is important to remember that the ancestral, family and constellation work offers a new point or perspective to move forward from and that it is ultimately the individuals choice and responsibility to move forward from that point and to leave their view or picture of the past behind.

The effects of war & religion with Derrick

Derrick's family are Swiss and he is currently working and travelling in Europe with no real base. Derrick had asked for a session because he felt like he didn't belong anywhere, he was constantly searching for "home"; he also had trouble establishing a financial base for himself as well as difficulty maintaining personal relationships. I spent some time working with Derrick and the energetic imprint of the family field and felt drawn to explore the Mother's family line in particular as it felt very disjointed and unsettled. We decided to set up a constellation to view the patterns *(Figure 9 - The Effects of War and Religion with Derrick (1).*

The Father was very detached and removed from the family. The first brother was very angry and directing a lot of that anger towards the Mother and Derrick. The second brother was more

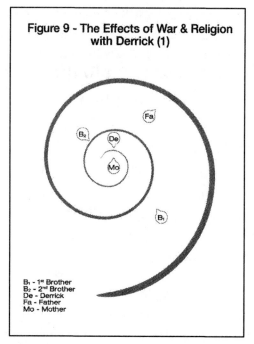

Figure 9 - The Effects of War & Religion
with Derrick (1)

B₁ - 1ˢᵗ Brother
B₂ - 2ⁿᵈ Brother
De - Derrick
Fa - Father
Mo - Mother

curious about Derrick and the Mother but couldn't see anyone else. The mother had difficulty seeing any of her children or her husband and was clearly drawn towards the realm of the dead. Derrick was very unsteady and weak in his place. As the Mother's line in particular had called to me at the start of the session I brought in representatives of the Mother's parents, Derrick's Grandparents. The Grandmother had little effect but introducing the Grandfather had an immediate and obvious effect on both Derrick and the Mother. It transpired that the Mother's Father's lines were Jewish and the Grandfather had been adopted in to a non-Jewish family during World War II in an attempt to save his life. This did save his life however his natural birth family perished in the holocaust. The Grandfather survived with his adopted family but went on to live a very bitter, violent and angry life. Both Derrick and his Mother were drawn to the victims surrounding the Grandfather in the realm of the dead whereas the eldest brother was drawn to the Grandfather himself. It seemed very clear that the Grandfather had been unable or had chosen not to show gratitude or honour the sacrifice his Mother and adoptive family had made in keeping him alive.

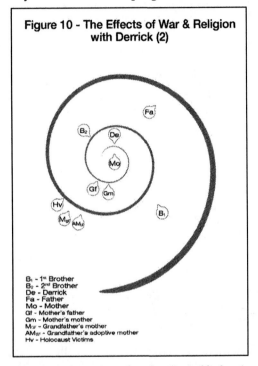

Figure 10 - The Effects of War & Religion with Derrick (2)

B₁ - 1ˢᵗ Brother
B₂ - 2ⁿᵈ Brother
De - Derrick
Fa - Father
Mo - Mother
Gf - Mother's father
Gm - Mother's mother
M_gf - Grandfather's mother
AM_gf - Grandfather's adoptive mother
Hv - Holocaust Victims

I brought in the representatives for the Grandfather's parents and adoptive family (*Figure 10 – The Effects of War and Religion with Derrick (2)*) and again this brought some relief to Derrick and his Mother, the Grandfather's parents still looked to the dead. I brought in representatives for the victims of the holocaust to stand beside them. It still remained impossible for the Grandfather to give thanks for his life and the sacrifices made. Derrick, during a very moving ceremony, was able to thank and honour the family members and victims, each in turn. He thanked them for their sacrifice and gave them a place of love in his heart. The grandfather was moved to stand with his Mother and the victims of the holocaust.

In doing so this freed Derrick's Mother and the balance within

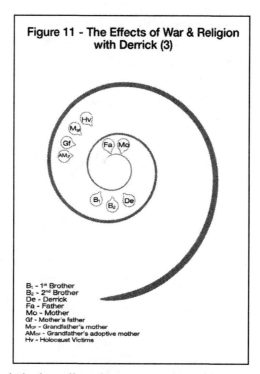

Figure 11 - The Effects of War & Religion
with Derrick (3)

B₁ - 1ˢᵗ Brother
B₂ - 2ⁿᵈ Brother
De - Derrick
Fa - Father
Mo - Mother
Gf - Mother's father
M₉ꜰ - Grandfather's mother
AM₉ꜰ - Grandfather's adoptive mother
Hv - Holocaust Victims

the family shifted to allow for a point of resolution to be reached. The three brothers were able to take their place in front of their parents who could also now see and be with one another (*Figure 11 - The Effects of War and Religion with Derrick (3)*).

The effects of the death of a sibling with Graham

Graham had requested a session because he said he felt quite lost with regards to what he was supposed to be doing professionally, he wasn't happy with his current profession and wanted out. He also went on to explain that his relationship with his Mother was not positive and that he felt she was a very negative and bitter woman. Again I spent some time working with Graham and the family lines and we decided to opt for a guided visualisation exploring the family lines as opposed to setting up the patterns spatially. Graham's energy felt like it was attempting to fill a space that was much too large for it, he felt as if he was also trying to bridge a distance between the male and female ancestors and that because of this he did not or could not have his rightful place in the family himself. We opted to focus on his family of origin and in particular the relationship with his Mother. It is interesting to note here that the relationship you have with your parents and in particular your Mother defines many things in your life. It also has an impact on your personal relationships and professional success. As Graham allowed himself to look upon and connect with his Mother's energy it became clear that she (the mother) could not see either Graham or his Father. She instead looked to the dead. It was also clear that she was looking towards a child that she had lost. When I suggested to Graham that there might be a sibling missing and asked him to try and bring this sibling in to his mind's eye he became very emotional. He suddenly recalled that his Mother had been pregnant when he was a young boy but that the baby, a boy, did not live for very long after he was born. Graham gained immense relief and peace from embracing his brother, giving him a place in his heart and acknowledging that he wasn't alone, there was another. We left the session at that point to continue on another day. We ended with Graham asking his brother to look upon him with love as his guardian. His sense of peace was tangible. It is always important to look to the children in the family and to look for the missing siblings. The other children, the surviving children, know that there is something missing on an unconscious level and they cannot fully take their place themselves in one or more of their siblings are excluded. This is also relevant for miscarriages, stillbirths and adoption but the effects can be particularly devastating with abortion; affecting the Mother and the relationship with the other siblings.

When siblings are excluded, an example with Liam

Relationships between siblings can be complicated at the best of times but become even more so when either or both parents remarry and have further children; this effect is compounded when the first relationship isn't given its proper place or acknowledged in an appropriate way. This was highlighted by an individual who came for a session because he was having trust issues both within his personal relationship and within his business. He ran a family business with his Father and also employed his sister. It became immediately apparent that he was very angry and that he was directing a lot of this anger towards his ex-wife and his sister, though neither of these two was the root cause of this anger.

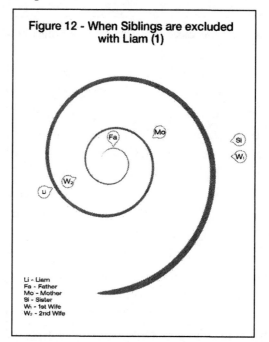

Figure 12 - When Siblings are excluded with Liam (1)

Li - Liam
Fa - Father
Mo - Mother
Si - Sister
W₁ - 1st Wife
W₂ - 2nd Wife

On setting up the patterns initially Liam became increasingly agitated and was behaving aggressively towards his sister's representative. He tried to force her to physically leave the room (and in effect forcing her from the family) and attempted to pull his Father over towards him. The Father clearly loved both and was trying to placate them both. The sister's representative crouched down and unsurprisingly expressed fear towards Liam (crouching down or kneeling within a constellation can be an indication of representing a child or representing an adult that is locked in a childhood event or trauma). Liam also appeared to be behaving in a childlike way. It became an obvious step to intuit that the root of their particular issue lay in a childhood incident involving them both as well as their Mother *(Figure 12 – When Siblings are Excluded, with Liam (1))*.

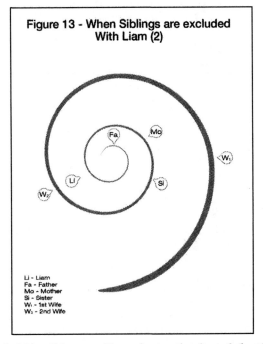

Figure 13 - When Siblings are excluded
With Liam (2)

Li - Liam
Fa - Father
Mo - Mother
Si - Sister
W₁ - 1st Wife
W₂ - 2nd Wife

I suggested this to Liam and he reluctantly shared that his (older) sister was in fact his stepsister, she wasn't actually his Father's daughter and that his Mother had been pregnant with her previous partner's child when she met Liam's father. The sister did not know any of this until Liam 'accidentally' let slip when they were young children that the man she thought was her Father was not indeed her Father, he was only Liam's Father, thus effectively excluding her from the family. There had been problems between the two siblings since that point and there continued to be problems within the business setting, as the sister was not allowed full access to the financial side of the business.

(Figure 13– When Siblings are Excluded, with Liam (2)).

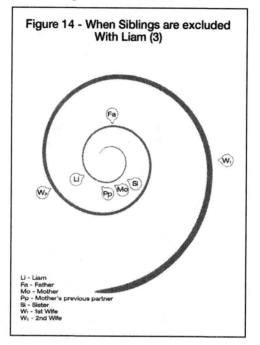

When Liam was placed opposite his sister he refused to look to her or to see her, he didn't listen to her saying 'please' and he simply could not say either 'I give you a place in this family'or'I acknowledge your place'. By adding in his Mother's previous partner we could see that it was with the two of them that his anger really lay. *(Figure 14– Liam's Spiral Constellation (3)).*

I placed Liam in front of the previous partner and allowed the two of them to look upon one another. Liam then said 'you are important for me' at this point some of his anger was released however he still refused to look upon either his Mother or his Sister *(Figure 15 – When Siblings are Excluded, with Liam(4)).* I chose to end the constellation at this point and instead gave Liam some simple visualisation exercises to try at home in the hope that when he was ready to see his family as it really is and not how he would choose it to be that he would be able to move forward.This sort of work is not a magical cure all, change has to be both

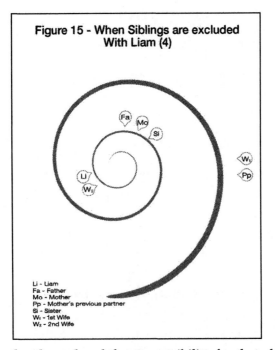

Figure 15 - When Siblings are excluded
With Liam (4)

Li - Liam
Fa - Father
Mo - Mother
Pp - Mother's previous partner
Si - Sister
W₁ - 1st Wife
W₂ - 2nd Wife

desired and embraced and the responsibility for that always lies with the individuals themselves. Liam completed further work with this but it was all done at a pace that he was comfortable with and when he felt ready to take the necessary steps.

A Family Secret with Isobel

Isobel came to see me because she felt that something heavy was being passed down the female line in the family. Upon spending some time working with her energy it did feel that the left side of her body was burdened however it also felt as if the right hand side of her body had areas that felt like holes, where people had 'disappeared'. I suggested that the male line in the family felt unstable and that at times it tried to make itself disappear, this can be an indication of addiction or drug/alcohol abuse in a line – particularly the male line. It is useful to note at this point that the Mother's line if often much clearer to intuit because of the link: Mother→Daughter→Daughter→Daughter and so on'The Father's line is in contrast naturally more branched or disjointed when it appears energetically. Isobel shared that her Father was an alcoholic and that the majority of the women in her Mother's line had married alcoholic and destructive men. Interestingly Isobel worked as a nurse with people suffering addiction abuse, very often those in the healing professions that deal with these issues (such as social workers, nurses etc) have had a family history of addictions abuse in the family and instead of allowing themselves to accept their Father (in most cases it is the male line) as their Father, even given all his entanglements and pain, they instead choose to seek this Fatherly connection by aiding and assisting those who are either suffering from addictions themselves or those that suffer indirectly. This is a path that leads to an eventual burn out as most social workers can attest to as they will never achieve what they set out to do – how can they if what they are unconsciously searching for lies within their own family and they look to others instead?

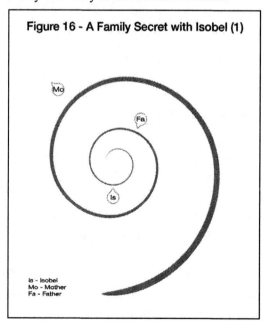

Figure 16 - A Family Secret with Isobel (1)

Is - Isobel
Mo - Mother
Fa - Father

Upon setting up the constellation it was clear that the Mother (who had died of Cancer) looked towards the dead, I also felt that there were siblings who needed to come forward (*Figure 16 – A Family Secret, with Isobel(1)*). When I suggested we initially bring in a younger sibling Isobel broke down. A younger sister had been stillborn when Isobel was a child and had been buried in an unmarked grave.Including this Sister and giving her a place lightened Isobel immediately. She was able to say: "*I am your big sister*" "*You are my little Sister*" "*I give you a place in my heart with much love*" Still it felt that another sibling was missing, when I suggested that there might be an older sibling Isobel suddenly "remembered" that he Father had a daughter from a previous relationship. They had not been married but did have a child together and then the Father went on to marry Isobel's Mother. The previous relationship wasn't spoken of within the family as it made Isobel's Mother uncomfortable. We brought in a representative for the older sister and her mother (*Figure 17– A Family Secret, with Isobel (2)*)

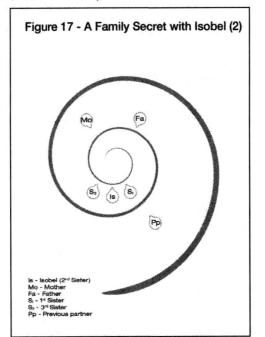

Figure 17 - A Family Secret with Isobel (2)

Is - Isobel (2ⁿᵈ Sister)
Mo - Mother
Fa - Father
S₁ - 1ˢᵗ Sister
S₂ - 3ʳᵈ Sister
Pp - Previous partner

Previous relationships have to be honoured and acknowledged or the children of the subsequent relationship will be drawn to or sympathise unconsciously with the first partner, this is also applicable if the children from the prior relationship are then excluded by one or other of the parents. Isobel was able to say:*"I respect your place in this family" "You are the first child, I am the second, and she is the third"*

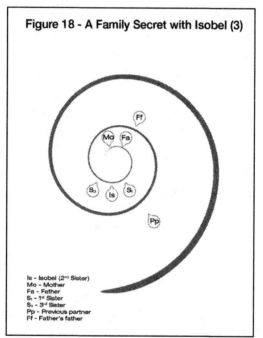

Figure 18 - A Family Secret with Isobel (3)

Is - Isobel (2ⁿᵈ Sister)
Mo - Mother
Fa - Father
S₁ - 1ˢᵗ Sister
S₃ - 3ʳᵈ Sister
Pp - Previous partner
Ff - Father's father

At this point Isobel's Mother was able to turn around from the dead and actually see her children. I also brought in a representative for Isobel's Father's Father to strengthen him and reconnect him with that line, as I briefly mentioned earlier alcoholism is often a long term suicide bid because someone (i.e. the father) is missing from the family field, in this case it was also compounded by the exclusion of the other two daughters (*Figure 18– A Family Secret with Isobel (3)*). We stopped the work at this point.Isobel continued to work on the relationship with her Father and her Father's ancestral line at a later point. This has great benefit for her own son who was strongly drawn to his maternal Grandfather.

The effects of concealed abuse with Julie

Julie came because she was very anxious, so much so that she rarely left the house (she had cancelled and rebooked her appointment many times before she actually managed to come). She had reclused herself after a series of damaging abusive relationships however she was now in a stable happy marriage but was still extremely anxious and did not like to interact with others. I spent some time working with her energetic field and explored the family lines allowing a picture of the situation to form in my head. I was very drawn to the female line and in particular to her Mother. The line felt very unstable and physically weak, it kept slipping from my view as if it were attempting to disappear itself or to leave. It felt very much like a line of pain. When I shared this with Julie she quietly explained that her Mother had been abused as a child by her Father (Julie's Grandfather). Her Grandmother and her Aunts had also had this experience. As a result of this her Mother had made attempts on her own life. Julie was now essentially being the Mother to her Mother and they had switched roles; this has the effect of disempowering the parent and keeping them trapped in their limbo-like situation, as the child attempts to take on their parent's fate in order to save them. It is worthwhile to note here that suicide and mental disturbance can be very strong repetitive patterns within the family lines and with the ancestors. It very often points to a traumatic, violent event, such as a murder, that an earlier ancestor has not taken responsibility for or acknowledged. It is therefore carried forward and perpetuated by future generations. The dead, the ancestors and the victims in these cases do not act as if they are dead; they still influence as if they are in the realm of the living. The individuals and events concerned need to be acknowledged in an appropriate way in order for the ancestors and indeed the victims to be at peace in the realm of the dead.

Figure 19 - The Effects of Concealed Abuse with Julie (1)

Mo - Mother
Ju - Julie

After some other work I set up a constellation for Julie and her Mother (*Figure 19 – The Effects of Concealed Abuse with Julie (1)*). Initially the two just looked at one another and stayed that way for a long time. Julie was able to say:*"You are my Mother""I am your daughter"*But she refused to hear her Mother say:*"You are only the child""I will carry my burdens myself"*Or to acknowledge in words herself that she was the child in the relationship. She refused to take her place as the child and to give her Mother her rightful place. Her Mother turned away and dropped to her knees (*Figure 20 – The Effects of Concealed Abuse with Julie (2)*).

Julie was too afraid to let go. She was afraid that he Mother would leave or commit suicide if she allowed her to be her Mother. The Mother was clearly drawn to the dead and to her own death. At this point we stopped the constellation and I did some further, individual work with Julie.Accepting the fates of others (as their own fates) as well as accepting your own fate can be challenging and humbling. To assume that you know better and to

Figure 20 - The Effects of Concealed
Abuse with Julie (2)

Mo - Mother
Ju - Julie

interfere with someone's fate, to not allow them to take their place, is a dangerous game and the effects of this will be experienced physically/emotionally/mentally/spiritually in your own life.

The immediate effects of Murder within the current generation, with Moira

Moira came to see me because her young five-year old son had been diagnosed as ADHD (Attention Deficit Hyperactive Disorder) and had been prescribed drugs to manage his condition, plus he also had difficulty sleeping. She was uncomfortable with the idea of managing her child with drugs and was open to other suggestions. The family history was complicated as she had married three times and had two older sons to two previous husbands. We set up a constellation and included the two previous partners.

As you can see (*Figure 21 – The immediate effects of Murder within the current generation, with Moira (1)*) the family's energy

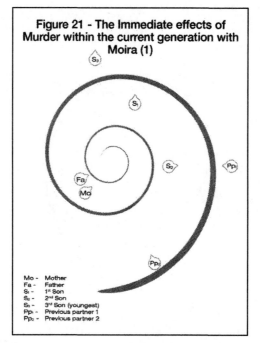

Figure 21 - The Immediate effects of Murder within the current generation with Moira (1)

Mo - Mother
Fa - Father
S₁ - 1ˢᵗ Son
S₂ - 2ⁿᵈ Son
S₃ - 3ʳᵈ Son (youngest)
Pp₁ - Previous partner 1
Pp₂ - Previous partner 2

was very scattered. The eldest son was very angry and agitated and seemed to be searching for something, the middle son was withdrawn and looked to the 1st husband instead of his own Father (which as I talked about previously often happens when previous relationships are not properly acknowledged within the family) The two previous partners however had little effect on the youngest son, instead he was obviously drawn to the dead. When I brought in a representative for the dead person the youngest and middle son were drawn to him immediately. The eldest son became highly agitated, however in contrast the youngest son lay down beside the dead representative. Given what I was seeing I asked Moira if a murder had been committed. She started to cry and explained that the eldest son had been involved in murdering a young man when she had been pregnant with her youngest son. He had been placed in a detention centre to await the court hearing along with the other boys involved in the murder however due to a technicality her son avoided prosecution and was released. The murder was never again referred to by the family and they moved away to another town. In these cases the murderer and the victim belong together, a bond exists between them and they are drawn to one another. The victim cannot be at peace in the realm of the dead unless he is acknowledged by the perpetrator, the murderer. If the murderer refuses to acknowledge the victim then very often someone else within the family or a future generation will attempt to atone for the murderer. This can show itself as a form of mental disturbance, in this case the youngest son was unconsciously attempting to atone for the actions of his elder brother, and he was 'sensing' the dead and could not be at peace until the victim was.

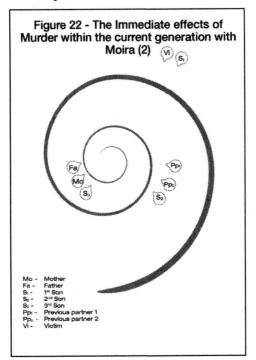

Figure 22 - The Immediate effects of Murder within the current generation with Moira (2)

Mo - Mother
Fa - Father
S₁ - 1st Son
S₂ - 2nd Son
S₃ - 3rd Son
Pp₁ - Previous partner 1
Pp₂ - Previous partner 2
Vi - Victim

I placed the eldest son with the victim (*Figure 22 – The immediate effects of Murder within the current generation, with Moira (2)*). He looked to the victim and simply said:*"You and I"*They looked upon one another for a long time and then both lay down, at peace. The youngest son and the Mother both bowed down in front of the victim to honour his sacrifice, they then returned to their place.It is amazing the things that are 'forgotten' or suppressed within a family, the secrets that are never spoken off, the children that never were, the affairs, the crimes, the violence, the murders, the abuse, the missing, the beloved. All the things that are swept under the carpet, the unseen, the unspoken has a habit of making itself heard further down the line, often we know what has gone before we have simply forgotten or chosen to forget.

Chapter 8

Back to the Realm of the Living

We have just begun to scratch the surface when it comes to working with the ancestors and the family lines. Now hopefully we can begin to see our family in a different context and not as something that exists purely to serve us. Rather like the discovery that the Earth revolves around the Sun and not the other way about. When we can see and fully appreciate the entanglements, events, struggles and achievements present in our family line, and our ancestors, we can start to really appreciate our own place within that great line. We can also hopefully go some way towards understanding why some things in our lives have come to be, why there are some patterns and issues that need addressed and a new way forward emerging. If we can appreciate that line of ancestors that we belong to and acknowledge it with love accepting it in to our hearts then we can draw the strength and wisdom from all those connected to it. The connection to the ancestors starts with our parents as well as our siblings (both born and unborn). If we can see and accept our parents, with all of their entanglements, and thank them for giving us this life then we can take a huge step forward in our own life. This is something that has to be done in the heart not the head. There is also the need to bring more honour once again to the role of the Father and the masculine line in general. The exclusion of the Father and of the masculine line has, I believe, contributed hugely to the prevalence of behavioural addictions and mood/depression disorders.If you think back to the exercise from chapter 4 where you were asked to write down any areas of your life that you feel blocked or that causes you pain, being as honest with yourself as you possibly could. Take a moment to look at your notes and think about how you felt.Now look at the notes you made of members of your immediate family that you grew up with and the brief history of their life that you described. The following spiral of influence *(Figure 23- Spiral constellation and realms of influence)* is for you to depict your own family patterns as you feel they are in the present moment. Place yourself and your immediate family members within the spiral. When you are ready place the "blocks" that you feel in your own life within the spiral too, whether the block or blocks are emotional, connected with your profession and success or a physical issue.

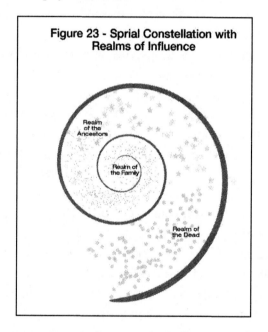

Figure 23 - Sprial Constellation with Realms of Influence

1. Close your eyes and allow your imagination to recreate your spiral in your mind's eye.
2. Spend a moment relaxing and focussing your awareness on your physical body. Allow your breath to flow naturally and quietly observe the sensations in your own body.
3. Focus on your feet, feel the surface upon which your feet rest. Visualise roots growing out of the centre of the soles of your

feet. Feel these roots burrowing through the floor upon which you are standing, through the foundations of the building, down into the earth. Imagine the roots growing deeper and deeper until they reach the centre of the earth. Feel yourself connected to the earth through your feet and then start to draw up the warm earth energy. Draw it up through your feet and feel it spiralling upwards through your body.

4. Now visualize your Root chakra as a red ball of light around the base of your spine. Feel the energy of the ball of light pulse there.

5. Now begin to gently tune in to this ball of red light in your mind. Noticing how it feels or affects the spiral of your family, any emotions or pictures that come to your mind's eye as you link in. Notice also if any other areas of your body draw your attention as you focus on your root.

6. Now turn your attention to your sacral chakra. Imagine a glowing, spinning orange coloured ball. Again noticing how it affects the family spiral, any emotions or pictures that come to your mind's eye as you link in. Relax and sink in to the experience.

7. When you are ready to move on bring your focus to your solar plexus chakra. You may see a glowing, spinning yellow coloured ball of light. How does this connect to your family spiral, what words, feelings or images are coming to you?

8. Now turn your attention to your heart chakra. This time the ball of light changes to a soft green colour. How do you feel connecting with this chakra? What if any emotions or pictures come to your mind's eye as you link in with this chakra and your ancestral spiral? Allow yourself to relax and breathe as you focus on your heart. You may sense that some chakras are quite restricted, and if need be, you can visualize them opening up, receiving energy from above until you are able to connect with them. You may also want to take some time to chant the "AH" mantra at this point.

9. When you are ready to move on bring your focus to your turn your attention to your solar plexus throat chakra. You will see a glowing, spinning blue coloured ball of light this time illuminating your spiral. Again noticing how it feels, any words, feelings or images that come to you. You may feel that you need to speak aloud at this point and if so it is important to allow yourself the space to do so.

10. Now turn your attention to your third eye chakra. Imagine a glowing, spinning brilliant indigo coloured light. Notice how it feels, any emotions or pictures that come to your mind's eye as you link in to your spiral. You may see images that seem familiar, allow yourself to relax and sink in to the experience.

11. When you are ready gently notice how the energy is moving upwards again and spreading to your crown chakra at the top of your head. You will see a pulsing ball of pure white of gold light. Notice how it feels, any emotions or pictures that come to your mind's eye as you link in. You may see images that seem familiar, allow yourself to relax and sink in to the experience you may find your thoughts wander to your children or the children within your family. See them within the Spiral and how they might become entangled.

12. Slowly bring your awareness back to your body, to your surroundings, wiggle your fingers and toes, and open your eyes gently.

Take some time to record your experience and note any areas that felt stuck or uncomfortable. Also take note of the areas or chakras where you felt you had a particularly strong or flowing connection and check back to Chapter 3 for the simple Chakra associations.

You have now highlighted some of the areas within your family and ancestral lines that are important to you and your family. You are now seeing the entanglements and the family members as they really are and where your place is in relation to where you belong. It is up to you to move forward from this point, to release the energy of resentment and desire to go back and change things. Acknowledge with deep respect and love what has gone before you, accept what is, take the family and ancestors in to your heart and create a new picture of the spiral to move forward from (*Figure 24 – New Spiral Constellation*).

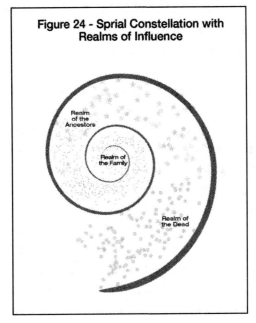

Figure 24 - Sprial Constellation with Realms of Influence

You may wish to light a candle to honour the ancestors that have gone before you and then simply say, 'I take my place'...

References

1. Roy, Nielson, Rylander et al. Family history of suicidal behaviour and earlier onset of suicidal behaviour. Psychiatry Research , Volume 129 , Issue 2 , Pages 217 - 219

2. William R Lovallo, Eldad Yechiam, Kristen H Sorocco, Andrea S Vincent, Frank L Collins (2006) Working Memory and Decision-Making Biases in Young Adults With a Family History of Alcoholism: Studies from the Oklahoma Family Health Patterns Project Alcoholism: Clinical and Experimental Research 30 (5) , 763–773

3. Nicola Mackay, Stig Hansen, Oona McFarlane. The Journal of Alternative and Complementary Medicine. December 1, 2004, 10(6): 1077-1081. doi:10.1089/acm.2004.10.1077

4. Fred Sicher & Elizabeth Targ et al. A Randomised Double-Blind Study of the Effect of Distant Healing in a Population with Advanced AIDS. West J Med. 1998 December; 169(6): 356–363.

5. Tim Duerden. An aura of confusion Part 2: the aided eye— 'imaging the aura?'. Complementary Therapies in Nursing and Midwifery. Volume 10, Issue 2, May 2004, Pages 116-123

6. Herbert Benson, The Relaxation Response. HarperTorch (August 1, 1976)

7. Shannahoff-Khalsa, DS, Bhajan, Y, The Healing Power of Sound: Techniques from Yogic Medicine. 4th International Symposium for Music in Medicine, Palm Springs, CA, Oct 24-29, 1989.

8. Werntz, DA, Bickford, RG, Bloom, FE, Shannahoff-Khalsa, DS, Alternating Cerebral Hemispheric Activity and the Lateralization of Autonomic Nervous Function. Human Neurobiology, (1983) 2:39-43.

9. Tomatis, A. A. "The Conscious Ear: My Life of Transformation through Listening." Station Hill Press, 1991.

10. Gilmore, Tim, The Efficacy of the Tomatis Method for Children with Learning and Communication Disorders: A Meta-Analysis, International Journal of Listening, Vol 13, 1999.

BOOKS

mySpiritRadio